youth MINISTRY

in the 21st century

the encyclopedia of practical ideas

revolutionary research
groundbreaking strategies
faith-building experiences

with **group** magazine editor **Rick Lawrence**

Group

Loveland, Colorado

www.group.com

Group resources actually work!

This Group resource helps you focus on **"The 1 Thing"**—a life-changing relationship with Jesus Christ. "The 1 Thing" incorporates our **R.E.A.L.** approach to ministry. It reinforces a growing friendship with Jesus, encourages long-term learning, and results in life transformation, because it's:

Relational
Learner-to-learner interaction enhances learning and builds Christian friendships.

Experiential
What learners experience through discussion and action sticks with them up to 9 times longer than what they simply hear or read.

Applicable
The aim of Christian education is to equip learners to be both hearers and doers of God's Word.

Learner-based
Learners understand and retain more when the learning process takes into consideration how they learn best.

Youth Ministry in the 21st Century: The Encyclopedia of Practical Ideas
Copyright © 2006 Group Publishing, Inc.
Foreword copyright © Christian Smith

Visit our Web site: **www.group.com**

Credits

Contributing Authors: Steve Argue, Rick Lawrence, Dave Livermore, Danette Matty, James W. Miller
Editor: Kate S. Holburn
Creative Development Editor: Mikal Keefer
Chief Creative Officer: Joani Schultz
Copy Editor: Jessica Broderick
Art Director: Jean Bruns
Book Designer: Granite Design
Print Production Artist: Joyce Douglas
Cover Art Director/Designer: Jeff A. Storm
Illustrators: Granite Design and Malwitz Design
Production Manager: Dodie Tipton

Unless otherwise indicated, all Scripture quotations are taken from the *Holy Bible,* New Living Translation, copyright © 1996, 2004. Used by permission of Tyndale House Publishers, Inc., Wheaton, Illinois 60189. All rights reserved.

Library of Congress Cataloging-in-Publication Data

Youth ministry in the 21st century : the encyclopedia of practical ideas.
     p. cm.
ISBN 0-7644-3076-9 (pbk. : alk. paper)
1. Church work with youth--Encyclopedias. I. Title: Encyclopedia of practical ideas.
BV4447.Y5845   2006
259' .23--dc22   2005023777
10 9 8 7 6 5 4 3 2 1   15 14 13 12 11 10 09 08 07 06
Printed in the United States of America.

Contents

113402

CHAPTER 3—Faith Expressed

CHAPTER 4—Spiritual Training

CHAPTER 5—Community-Building

Chapter 6—Parents

Chapter 7—Outreach and Evangelism

CHAPTER 8—Postmodernism

Contributors

Many thanks to the following people for their thoughtful and innovative contributions to this volume.

Steve Argue, M.Div., is the executive director of the Contextual Learning Center at Grand Rapids Theological Seminary, developing residency opportunities for graduate students seeking to serve in ministry. He is co-founder of Intersect, a regular contributor to Group Magazine, a trainer for Group Magazine Live, and a speaker to students around the country. He received his Master of Divinity from Trinity International University and his Bachelor in Business Administration in finance and marketing from the University of Wisconsin–Madison. Steve and his wife, Jenny, have three daughters, Kara, Elise, and Lauren, and live in Grand Rapids, Mich.

Rick Lawrence is the editor of Group Magazine and the executive editor in charge of Group Publishing's youth ministry training events (including Group Magazine Live) and two Web sites—www.groupmag.com and www.ministryandmedia.com. He is the author or co-author of hundreds of magazine articles and books, including *The Family-Friendly Church* and *TrendWatch*. He is married to Beverly Rose and has two daughters, Lucy Rose and Emma Grace.

Dave Livermore, Ph.D., is executive director of the Global Learning Center at Grand Rapids Theological Seminary and is co-founder of Intersect, a ministry that provides leadership training and consulting to emerging leaders in ministries around the world. Dave has authored two books, numerous articles, and training manuals. He has a heart for the globe and has had the opportunity to serve with national leaders in more than 50 countries. Dave and Linda Livermore live in Grand Rapids, Mich., with their two daughters, Emily and Grace.

Danette Matty is an 18-year youth ministry volunteer, freelance writer, and speaker, as well as contributing editor for The Source For Youth Ministry. She and her husband, Eric, serve as associate pastors of Real Life Church in Roseville, Minnesota. Danette teaches, hangs out, and laughs a lot with teenagers in C.R.E.W. Youth Ministries, as well as with her own two kids—her all-time favorite students.

Jim Miller is the associate pastor for student ministries at the First Presbyterian Church of Honolulu. He and his wife, Yolanda, have been serving in youth ministry for almost a decade. Jim is a graduate of Princeton Seminary and the University of California, Berkeley.

Special thanks to **Christian Smith** for his vision, generosity, and pioneering efforts in researching youth, and specifically for writing the foreword to this volume. He is the National Study of Youth and Religion's lead researcher and driving force and is the Stuart Chapin Distinguished Professor and associate chairman for the department of sociology at the University of North Carolina at Chapel Hill. He received his Master of Arts and Ph.D. from Harvard University's Graduate School of Arts and Sciences (department of sociology). He is also the author of *Soul Searching: The Religious and Spiritual Lives of American Teenagers* (Oxford University Press, 2005).

Foreword by Christian Smith

What is the National Study of Youth and Religion, and why should youth leaders pay attention to its findings?

In short, the NSYR is the most extensive and detailed national research study on the religious and spiritual lives of U.S. teenagers to date, providing a depth of knowledge and understanding about the religious lives of U.S. adolescents that was simply not available previously. Such knowledge and understanding provide a good basis for informed reflection and discussion in many communities—especially communities of faith—concerned with the lives of teenagers in the United States today.

It Started in 2000

In 2000, while considering the idea of studying adolescent religion in the United States, I was surprised to discover how little reliable research had been conducted on youth religion at a national level. I came across some existing surveys about teenage religion with relatively small samples and methodologies that seemed questionable. I also found some good general adolescent surveys, but they included only a few questions about religion.

In the end, it seemed nobody had the broad social scientific knowledge about the religious and spiritual lives of U.S. teenagers I had expected would be available and many people's apparent interest in the matter seemed to warrant.

In response to that lack of knowledge, the Lilly Endowment generously granted an award to conduct a national research study of U.S. adolescent religion, giving birth to the NSYR (www.youthandreligion.org). In the spring and summer of 2003, after a year and a half of preparation, the NSYR conducted a national telephone survey with 3,370 teen-parent pairs from around the United States.

Respondents were chosen with a random-digit-dialing method, assuring a nationally representative sample of teenagers and their parents.

Research science has demonstrated that if a sample size is large enough and the selection of respondents is random—as is the case with the random-digit-dialing method—then responses from the sample will be nearly identical to the responses one would get from the entire population, that is, to what (in this case) every teenager and parent in America would say. The NSYR followed exactly this kind of careful methodology, so its findings can be assumed to accurately represent all the teenagers in the United States.

Interviews With Real Teenagers

In each case, a 30-minute (average) survey was conducted with one parent and a 52-minute (average) survey was conducted with a teenager randomly chosen from the household. The survey—which was conducted in English and Spanish as needed—gathered an immense amount of information on U.S. teenagers' religious affiliations, beliefs, identities, experiences, practices, commitments, activities, congregations, and expected futures.

The survey also collected a large amount of data about the teens' families, relationships with parents, schools, friends, neighborhoods, moral attitudes and actions, risk behaviors, dating and sexual experiences, emotional well-being, social ties to adults, and much more.

No other existing national survey of teenagers comes close to having the detail of information on these aspects of U.S. adolescents' lives, particularly their religious lives.

Next Steps

In order to follow up on the telephone survey with a complementary research methodology, members of the NSYR research team conducted personal, in-depth interviews with 267 teenagers from 45 different states, sampled from among the survey respondents. These 267 interview subjects were sampled to achieve diversity of religious type, regional location, gender, age, race, school type, and family structure. In these interviews—conducted privately and confidentially, mostly in libraries and restaurants in teens' hometowns—teenagers were able to describe and explain in much greater depth than they could for the survey about their religious faith, spiritual practices, life experiences, thoughts, beliefs, feelings, and hopes.

In these interviews, we were able to gain much greater depth and nuance of understanding of the teens' lives, yet in a way that their responses connected back to their original survey answers in order to directly link quantitative and qualitative data. (For details on the survey and interview methodologies, see www.youthandreligion.org/research/.)

Essential Insight for Youth Leaders

The broad scope and scale of the NSYR's effort in researching the religious and spiritual lives of U.S. teenagers is unprecedented and therefore important for people who work with adolescents. The survey and interview data together provide a wealth of information on an enormous variety of subjects, all connected to a new and unparalleled body of nationally representative research data on teenagers' religious and spiritual lives.

As a result, scholars are now able to use solid empirical evidence to test their prior observations, evaluate their hypotheses, confirm their hunches, and generally expand the body of reliable knowledge about U.S. adolescents' lives.

Parents, youth leaders, ministry organizations, and churches should thus be better able to understand their teenagers and work on more well-informed relationships with and practices and programs for the teenagers in their midst.

The NSYR's first major findings are now available in the book *Soul Searching: The Religious and Spiritual Lives of American Teenagers* (by Christian Smith with Melinda Lundquist Denton, Oxford University Press, 2005). Refer to this book for more in-depth reporting on the project and the findings on which this book reflects and to which it responds.

The Purpose of the NSYR

The National Study of Youth and Religion does not exist to tell people what to do with its findings. It is the job of the users—and not the providers—of such research to consider what the findings may mean in their particular situations. The NSYR exists rather to provide reliable sociological data and to support informed and hopefully constructive conversations about teenagers' real lives.

The NSYR's Impact for Youth Leaders

Clearly, among faith communities in the United States, the implications of NSYR findings will vary from one faith tradition, denomination, and congregation to another. For those parents, communities, and ministries concerned with the lives of U.S. adolescents—particularly with their religious and spiritual lives—the NSYR offers a wealth of new and reliable information to dig into, contemplate, discuss, and respond to.

Perhaps especially important to consider is our finding, described in *Soul Searching*, that the de facto, functional religion of the majority of U.S. teenagers is an inter-religious faith that I call "Moralistic Therapeutic Deism" (see more on page 15). This and other significant findings will most likely strongly impact the way youth leaders carry out ministry to teenagers.

In any case, we hope that, in the end, NSYR findings contribute to both improved lives for U.S. teenagers and improved relationships between teenagers and those responsible for their emotional and spiritual well-being.

Using This Resource

Welcome to *Youth Ministry in the 21st Century: The Encyclopedia of Practical Ideas.*

The National Study of Youth and Religion offers revolutionary, never-seen-before insight about American teenagers' lives and faith (see study details on pages 10-12). Some of the results are alarming, some encouraging, and all fascinating to people passionate about helping youth grow close to Jesus. We picked eight specific conclusions that are absolutely crucial for youth leaders to discover and apply in their ministries. And you'll have the opportunity to do both as you explore the eight chapters of this volume.

Each chapter has two parts. The first section "unpacks" the conclusion topic at hand (this tells you why the study finding is significant and matters to you). The second section, called "Ministry Tools," provides practical tools for applying the finding (this gives you great ideas for answering the question "So what can I do about this in my ministry?").

The "Ministry Tools" sections will give you more than **100 ideas** for events, games, small groups, worship, discussion starters, object lessons, the arts, all-church experiences, outreach, affirmation, service, reflection, overall strategy...and on and on. You'll see the "OK to copy" icon on pages where you'll distribute copies either to individual students or to groups.

We know that through this volume you'll see your teenagers' spiritual lives in a new light and understand who they really are with a fresh perspective. We also know you'll gain valuable, practical, and innovative ideas that will inspire your students to a life-transforming relationship with the Messiah and King.

Our prayer is that this tool will encourage you and strengthen your ministry as you serve God by loving youth. May God work through you and your ministry in ways you can't yet even imagine.

—*Kate Holburn, Editor*

Chapter 1

THE BASICS OF Faith

Back to the Basics
by Rick Lawrence

When most teenagers think of God, they think of someone who looks a lot like a "Divine Butler." So says Dr. Christian Smith, lead researcher for the National Study of Youth and Religion. Smith says today's teenagers treat their Christian faith as "instrumental," meaning that God exists to help us do what we want because he fundamentally wants us to be happy. Smith gives this mind-set a name—"Moralistic Therapeutic Deism."

It's an umbrella term used to describe a parasite that's embedded itself in every major religion, not just Christianity. If **Moralistic** (life is all about making right and wrong choices; the goal is to be a good person who exhibits good morals) **Therapeutic** (God exists for our pleasure, not the other way around; faith in God is important because God helps us get what we want) **Deism** (although God exists, he is an essentially unknowable lawgiver; we can't have a relationship with him because he's distant, although "on call" to fix problems) is broken down to its core, it basically means our teenagers don't understand the basics of the gospel, the person of Jesus, or the role God *really* wants to play in their lives.

This means we're privileged to be leaders who get to reintroduce "the greatest story ever told" to a generation of young people who've forgotten it.

Do We Know Jesus Well Enough to Know What He'd Do?

When the "What Would Jesus Do?" movement was hot, I felt a deep unrest about its foundations. Though the WWJD craze was sparked by Charles Sheldon's book *In His Steps,* it never answered the primary question posed by Sheldon in his book: "If Christians are supposed to be following Jesus, why aren't they making more of an impact in their daily lives?"

WWJD assumes we know Jesus well enough to make an educated guess as to what he'd do in any given situation. And I don't think we do.

The overwhelming evidence from the NSYR proves that we habitually forget the person we're supposed to be following.

We're Habitual Forgetters

We Christ followers don't have a great track record in remembering who Jesus really is. And this isn't simply a second-millennium problem—since the dawn of man, we've been fantastic forgetters. There's proof in Genesis 3:1-11.

> "The serpent was the shrewdest of all the wild animals the Lord God had made. One day he asked the woman, 'Did God really say you must not eat the fruit from any of the trees in the garden?'
>
> " 'Of course we may eat fruit from the trees in the garden,' the woman replied. 'It's only the fruit from the tree in the middle of the garden that we are not allowed to eat. God said, "You must not eat it or even touch it; if you do, you will die." '
>
> " 'You won't die!' the serpent replied to the woman. 'God knows that your eyes will be opened as soon as you eat it, and you will be like God, knowing both good and evil.'
>
> "The woman was convinced. She saw that the tree was beautiful and its fruit looked delicious, and she wanted the wisdom it would give her. So she took some of the fruit and ate it. Then she gave some to her husband, who was with her, and he ate it, too."

You know the rest of the story.

Let's take a closer look at what happened here. When Satan first approached Eve, he seeded doubt about God's clear instructions to her.

At first, Eve responded well—she repeated what God had said to her. But then Satan questioned God's character, intentions, and nature. The core of his deceit was simply that God is not who he says he is.

And in that moment, Eve forgot God, kick-starting something that's now deep in our DNA: a deep-down suspicion of God and a willingness to forget what he's really like.

That's why the people of God have long been locked into a "cycle of forgetting." We start out faithful to God, then slowly forget him, then descend into sin, then experience God's discipline, then begin to remember him again, then return to faithfulness. This cycle has repeated itself over and over—impacting even the giants of our faith.

The last epistle Paul wrote before he was martyred was 2 Timothy. The book is full of "fatherly advice" as Paul tells Timothy what matters most. Together, Paul and Timothy had endured harsh beatings, imprisonments, shipwrecks...you name it. And they did all of it for the love of Jesus.

That's why Paul's advice in 2 Timothy 2:8-9a is so...shocking: "Always remember that Jesus Christ, a descendant of King David, was raised from the dead. This is the Good News I preach. And because I preach this

Good News, I am suffering and have been chained like a criminal."

Why would Paul remind Timothy to remember Jesus? Perhaps because Paul knew that no matter how much we love and know Jesus, we tend to forget him. It's the cycle of forgetting in operation. And the results of the NSYR make it easy to see that cycle still playing itself out in our midst.

Smith's results show us that most American teenagers are "functional Deists"—they believe in a God who exists and created the world, but, other than being "on call" in times of stress or need, that God is not particularly involved in the world or their own personal lives in a very meaningful or important way.

Not long ago, a woman who leads a small group for sixth-grade girls told me she's been listening to how her girls talk about their relationships with God—they treat him as an "important accessory" in their lives. That is, it's important to wear the right clothes, listen to the right music, watch the right TV shows, and worship the right God.

That's not the gospel of Jesus. Jesus discipled his followers into relationships with God that were all-consuming—they were supposed to be the *hub* of their everyday lives, not the *hubcap*.

At some point, if we really want to teach teenagers to "do what Jesus did," we have to ask ourselves how well they know the basics of their faith. For example, a fast journey through Matthew's Gospel reveals that...

- Jesus spent an astonishing amount of time praying—and much of that time appears to be spent in what we might call "spiritual warfare." He knew his followers were in a fight with a serious foe whose goal was to "steal and kill and destroy" them (like the thief in John 10:10). What's more, when he sent his disciples out on their own for the first time, he explicitly told them to "cast out demons."

- Jesus enjoyed spending time with desperate, avowed sinners because they were honest enough about themselves to know they needed God.

- Jesus said our goal in following him should be to deliver the gospel well enough to cause some people to insult, defame, and persecute us.

- Jesus hated religious rule keeping and took every opportunity he could to break man-made rules for the purpose of highlighting God's deeper truths.

- Jesus told his followers to plunge themselves into the darkness—the mainstream culture—because they were meant to be light. He was not describing a warm 60-watt bulb; he expects us to be spotlights.

- Jesus talked matter-of-factly about hell and bluntly warned that there are terrible consequences waiting for those who reject God's grace and mercy.

- Jesus hated it when people prayed or served or sacrificed to bolster their identity or inflate their ego—he advised his followers to express the truth of their love for God by doing great things in secret.

- Jesus was quick to forgive those who were repentant and quick to blast those who weren't.

- Jesus said the richest people were those who gave the most relative to what they had. He advised his followers that if their ties to earthly possessions were so strong that they overshadowed their allegiance to him, they'd be better off giving away all their stuff.

- Jesus told us to study what people do more than what people say.

- Jesus made sick, crippled, and terminally ill people well.

- Jesus loved a good party, apparently throwing himself into celebrations with such abandon that some religious people thought he was a drunkard.

- Jesus told us we actually have to go out and "harvest" new believers by telling the good news of God's grace—we can't wait around for "fruit" to detach itself from the tree and hurl itself at us.

- Jesus said our loyalty to him should outweigh our loyalty to our family, friends, and workplace relationships.

- Jesus told us not to focus our energies on fighting sin in others (pulling weeds) but instead to encourage good growth in others (growing wheat).

- Jesus said the root of our unbelief is our astonishing ability to forget who God is and what he's done. That's why he tells and retells God's story in every conceivable form and then urges us to pursue that story every day.

Clearly, the NSYR shows that these basic ideas of who Jesus is and what he's about haven't gotten through to our teenagers. This means that whatever strategies we're using to help our teenagers understand the basics of our faith simply aren't working.

Why Our Strategies for Teaching Faith Basics Are Failing

What we've tried so far to teach our teenagers the most important truths hasn't transformed them enough to seep into their everyday lives—at least that's what researchers with the NSYR discovered over and over.

Our teaching hasn't effectively bridged the gap between biblical truth and everyday realities.

A popular bumper sticker reads, "If Jesus is the answer, what's the question?" We're basically answering questions that teenagers haven't raised. Their *real* questions are all about the pragmatic realities that disturb, confuse, and dishearten them.

For example…

- "Is it my fault my parents are splitting up?"
- "If I agree to have sex with my boyfriend, will that get me the unconditional love I crave?"
- "If I pray hard enough, will God help me play so well that our team will win?"

We treat the Bible's truths as if they're divorced from everyday realities when our job is to build bridges between the Bible and teenagers' *real* world.

We haven't battled the "everyone's right" mentality well.

One of the strongest themes in postmodern life is pluralism: It's great to be passionate about your "truth" as long as you don't put down or negate my "truth." It's well-accepted in our culture—and in Christian culture—that there are many paths leading to God.

But Jesus just didn't allow for that option. He said there is only one "shepherd" (that would be him)—the rest are "hired hands." He said there are only one gate and one path (again, him) that lead to life—and the other gates and paths lead to blind cliffs.

Culturally acceptable or not, one basic of the Christian faith is the reality of "exclusionary truths."

To help his teenagers grasp the consequences of Jesus' exclusionary claims, longtime youth minister Kent Julian shows teenagers a fishbowl with a live fish in it. Julian asks teenagers to imagine what it must be like to be that fish—always hemmed in by the narrow confines of the bowl.

"Doesn't this fish deserve freedom?" Julian asks. When teenagers respond with "yes," he carefully extracts the fish from the bowl and puts it on the floor.

It doesn't take long for the teenagers to start demanding that Julian put the struggling fish back in the fishbowl. He then helps teenagers make comparisons between the fishbowl and God's "only one gate, only one path" truths.

Jesus said, "I am the way, the truth, and the life. No one can come to the Father except through me" (John 14:6). This is a crucial truth that's at odds with the deep flow of teenagers' moral culture. And the first step toward addressing this conflict is counterintuitive: We must highlight the differences between the gospel of Jesus Christ and every other popular spiritual path. Teenagers must first understand that *all* paths are not *one* path.

There are many ways to discover the basic tenets of the world's major religions and alternate "truths" (for example, scientology). Take your teenagers on a field trip to a mosque, temple, or meeting place; then debrief the experience with them immediately after. Involve students in researching the foundational beliefs of the world's alternate belief systems.

The key here is to plunge teenagers into these false belief systems and help them understand the unique claims of Christ. For example, no figure in any world religion other than Christianity claims deity—all others are self-described prophets and truth tellers, but not God.

We haven't addressed teenagers' cynicism toward the church.

One faith basic is the reality that a teenager's relationship with the local church matters.

Spanish youth minister Luis Mellado wrote a piece in a National Network of Youth Ministries e-newsletter describing the similarities he's noticed between the young Samuel of the Bible and today's Christian teenagers—teenagers who often see the church through the same cynical lens as their secular peers. Samuel faced similar forces that worked against him embracing the truth, but he overcame them and didn't become cynical.

Here are some insights about Samuel's experience with the church:

- **Samuel didn't have a choice about going to church.** His mother dedicated Samuel to God before he was born (1 Samuel 1:11). Samuel was taken to church and actually *lived* there! Some teenagers may resent growing up in church, but this didn't keep Samuel from embracing his religious heritage.

- **Samuel grew up in a society that had fallen away from God.**
  "Now in those days messages from the Lord were very rare, and
  visions were quite uncommon" (1 Samuel 3:1b). Teenagers are
  growing up in a secularized society that is moving to the post-
  Christian era. Many of them are on the inside looking out, feeling they're missing something. They are attracted to the world.
  The temptations and opportunities that the world offers them can
  seem too great to resist. But Samuel resisted.

- **Samuel grew up in a church filled with double standards and
  hypocrisy.** Eli's sons were priests, but they were corrupt (1
  Samuel 2). As children become adolescents, they're able to see
  the weaknesses and mistakes of their parents and leaders, and
  this can lead to a deep cynicism about the church. Samuel didn't
  fall prey to this temptation.

- **Although Samuel grew up in church, he didn't really know God
  (1 Samuel 3:7).** Samuel knew the songs and the Scriptures. He
  knew *about* God, but he didn't yet *know* God; there was no *relationship* with God. God was calling Samuel, and Samuel didn't
  recognize God's voice.

Mellado says the key to what made the difference in Samuel's life lies
in the first verse of chapter 3: "Meanwhile, the boy Samuel served the
Lord by assisting Eli."

As Samuel committed himself to serving God, he stopped going through
the motions—cynically keeping his distance—and started relating to God.
He listened more than he questioned and acted more than he talked.

We no longer teach faith basics the way Jesus taught them.

For 30 years at Group Publishing, we've studied how young people
learn God's truths, and we know learning happens best when teaching is
relational, experiential, applicable, and learner-based (we call it R.E.A.L.
learning).

The best teaching is infused with time for discussion and interaction.
Teenagers learn best when they're involved in activities and they can make
a strong connection to their everyday lives.

We'll cover the R.E.A.L. approach at greater length in chapter 4.

What We Can Do to Build Faith Basics in Teenagers

We must decide whether our goal is to teach teenagers to be disciples of Jesus. If we say yes, then we're well-served to teach truth to teenagers by emulating how Jesus did it.

Get simple.

Simple doesn't mean shallow. The most knowledgeable people on the face of the earth are specialists. After I tore up my knee playing basketball, two physicians and two athletic trainers assured me there was no damage.

A year later, an orthopedic specialist operated on my knee to repair a torn ligament. He'd figured out what was wrong with me in 30 seconds.

The point: We have to narrow our focus to gain depth of knowledge and wisdom. We're covering way too much ground with our students instead of going deep with a handful of important truths.

When Jesus wanted to teach about God's forgiveness, the folly of pleasure seeking, the role of suffering in repentance, the place of extravagant celebration in our lives, and the fruitlessness of envy, he told one simple story—that of the Prodigal Son.

Unlike Jesus, we often teach our students to be generalists—people who know a smattering about a lot of things. When they enter into the wider culture to do battle over the claims of the gospel, they're quickly outmatched.

We must determine "The Five Most Important Truths" our students need to know and make sure they know those truths by the time they leave our ministry.

At a workshop several years ago, I asked youth leaders to develop a list of faith basics their students should know by the time those students leave the group. Here's a summary of the faith basics they identified:

- the plan of salvation/grace
- God loves me/Christ died for me
- how the Bible applies to my life
- how to pray
- understanding the faith
- traditions and rituals of the church and their meanings
- how to introduce others to Christ
- actions speak louder than words
- key Scriptures and understandings—John 3:16 and Ephesians 2:8-9, for example

I suggest you divide youth into small groups of three or more and challenge them to agree on the five most important, basic truths of the Christian faith. Gather back together and ask small groups to report; then challenge the group to synthesize all the suggestions into a final set of five truths.

You'll learn a *lot* by hearing what your students consider faith basics. Compare their list to your own. How closely do the items match?

Invite your senior pastor to a group meeting to give input. See if the pastor will take the final list and create a sermon series around it.

Get purposeful.

Jesus had a plan for spreading the gospel, and we need one, too.

The SonLife organization has developed a plan by identifying four stages of ministry in Jesus' disciple making. According to this plan, a disciple-making youth ministry does the following:

Builds—It first helps believers deepen their love relationship with Jesus and his church.

Equips—It then helps young people gain skills and experience in peer care.

Wins—It then helps young people gain skills and experience in peer evangelism.

Multiplies—Finally, it helps release potential shepherds to start the process all over again (the church-planting phase).

We can also build apologetics into the DNA of our ministries. For example…

- **Do a book study.** Many youth leaders have told us they use resources to get teenagers wrestling with biblical truths. Try these (and see the appendix on pages 222-223 for more great resources from Group Publishing):

  ▣ *Jesus—the LifeChanger* (Group Publishing)

  ▣ *Searching for the Truth* (Group Publishing)

  ▣ *A Fresh Start* (Group Publishing)

- **Create a summer "basic training" group.** Advertise it as a group for "the few, the proud." Use the summer flexibility to compare Christian beliefs with those of other faiths, to help teenagers practice telling the gospel story in the marketplace, to explore biblical truths through feature films, or to do a "harmony of the Gospels" study.

- **Create a "challenge question" that's tied to one of your five most important truths.** Use the last 10 minutes of your meeting time every week to challenge teams to be the first to answer the question with biblical backup. Here's an example: "True or false? The Bible teaches that though the best way to heaven is faith in Christ, there are other ways that work as well." After you crown the winning team, you can reiterate the core truth the team proved.

Get real.

Jesus didn't talk about faith fundamentals in distant, hypothetical ways. He almost always connected truth to story or everyday life.

To teach about the hierarchy of God's law versus man's law, Jesus broke a well-known Jewish law by picking wheat on the Sabbath. To teach about God's provision, he pointed to a bird in a tree. To teach about God's justice, Jesus used a familiar illustration about a farmer hiring workers at different times during the day but paying the same to each.

Communicate to teenagers that Jesus is rooted in history but relevant to their life stories by…

- **Using cultural tools to teach biblical truths.** Simply put, instead of fighting the cultural influences that are bombarding our students, let's teach students to think critically and biblically instead. That means using movies, music, news stories, video games, and television shows to spark conversations with teenagers about biblical truth.

  We need to not see pop culture as something about which we must always warn students but as raw material to engage students' hearts and minds. Let's guide students so they discover the fallacies undergirding some cultural influences and then help students compare those fallacies to God's great truths.

- **Inviting non-Christians to tell their stories to your students and then debriefing those stories.** Veteran youth minister Len Kageler has students listen to reasons why a speaker has decided *against* Christ, thank the speaker for sharing, and then wrestle with what they heard after the person leaves.

- **Brainstorming the "parables" in life.** Your life is telling God's story, too. The best time to recognize the "parables" in your life is when you're preparing to teach teenagers. Ask God how he's using the circumstances of your life to help you learn his truths. Then use those personal parables in your teaching—but make sure you bridge them back to biblical truth.

- **Taking more trips.** Our studies have shown that trips plunge teen-agers into real-life quandaries, decisions, and challenges better than any other single strategy. You need a steady stream of teach-able moments, and the hassles that happen on a trip are a great source. Nothing inspires prayer quite like being in trouble, and prayer calls our bluffs and forces us to decide if God is real.

Model It

In the end, our students learn faith basics through an unsettling filter—us.

Not long ago, I asked an online community of youth workers to tell me how they teach their teenagers about spiritual truths. Nearly 500 voted, and "role modeling" was their No. 1 response.

So what are your students learning about faith basics from studying your relationships and life?

Give them more to chew on by sampling the great ideas that follow.

Study, Schmudy

As you've just read, the National Study of Youth and Religion suggests that teenagers understand very little about the basics of the Christian faith and the Bible. Their lack of knowledge *also* extends to particulars of church tradition and denominations.

So it's pretty much a one-two punch: They don't understand the specifics, and they *also* don't understand foundational truths.

Ouch.

Two things to keep in mind as you address this knowledge void in the students who you serve in ministry:

First, the more you connect real life with faith basics, the more your students will engage and grapple with truth and be changed by what they discover. The ideas presented below stress involvement, relationship, and application through debriefing. That's no coincidence: Those elements guarantee involvement, and your students *must* be involved before learning can happen.

Second, if you want to fix a lack of education, it's important that you provide…well, education.

Your youth group needs more than games and general discussion—you've got to deliver content, too. And hear this: Your teenagers want and *need* content. The faith basics they're missing require that you (and, in a larger sense, your church and your teenagers' families) provide information.

How you go about delivering information is a critical concern. During a good part of the church's history, children memorized "catechisms," or long lists of questions and answers that communicated information. In Jesus' day, young *talmidim*, students of a rabbi, would memorize large portions of Scripture.

The problem with mastering facts is that facts alone don't provide a relationship with God. Make your goal to provide needed, important, relevant information in the context of *relationship*….a relationship with you and with God.

The activities you find in this book will help you accomplish just that.

[GAME IDEA]

I'll Take High School for 100

This activity can help you determine what level of understanding your students have of faith basics.

Create a Jeopardy-style game by drawing on various school subjects: Math, English, and history are good. Add columns relating to Bible factoids (such as being able to recite all of the Beatitudes) and to actual basics—the essentials of the faith, such as Jesus being God's Son.

As you play, pay attention to see if one of two patterns develop:

1. Your students are clueless about both Bible trivia and faith basics. If this is the case, it's possible they've been exposed to very little Bible teaching—or the Bible teaching they've experienced hasn't "stuck."

2. Your students are great with trivia but not so hot with faith basics. This pattern might indicate that while they're factually informed, they're not relationally connected to God. Not the ideal situation.

Create the game by writing questions in the following categories on the back of sheets of colored paper: Basic Math, English Literature, American History, Bible Facts, and Faith Basics.

Place the sheets on the wall in columns of five, with the questions taped toward the wall. On the back of the sheets, facing out, write dollar amounts: $100, $200, $300, and so on.

Use questions you'd expect an average high school student to know, but make the questions challenging. The goal isn't to stump students, but you won't learn much unless you discover what students *don't* already know, too.

Select the questions about faith basics carefully. What are the faith basics you most want kids to know in your ministry? See the survey results on page 22 to see what other youth ministers identified as relevant issues to raise.

Play the game by having students form two groups. Teams will take turns calling out a dollar amount in a certain column and then working together to suggest the correct answer. If a team gets the right answer, it scores that dollar amount and takes another turn.

continued on next page >>

I'll Take High School for 100
(continued)

When you've run out of questions, ask students to form pairs and discuss the following:

▣ **Of the columns on the wall, which are most important? Why?**

▣ **If you could be an expert in just one area, which would you select? Why?**

After students have shared for a few minutes, continue.

> SAY: **You probably get tested in some of these subject areas regularly. Math, English, and history are content areas you normally must master to graduate from high school.**
>
> **But Bible knowledge? That's typically not a high school prerequisite.**
>
> **And faith basics? They're probably not on your academic radar at all, yet they're vitally important. Knowing that Jesus is God's Son is huge, and being in a relationship with him is life-changing. So are the other truths you uncovered in the faith basics column.**
>
> **You'll deepen your appreciation about math the rest of your life. Don't believe me? Wait until you overcharge a checking account or max out a credit card. Life provides *ample* opportunities to keep developing math skills!**
>
> **Deepening spiritually requires you to focus on learning the basics and then letting God help apply them in your life. That process isn't always quite so automatic; it often requires a deliberate effort.**
>
> **And that's an effort we'll make together here in our group.**

[LARGER CHURCH CONNECTION]

The Membership Pledge

Invite to your group the person who teaches the new members' class at your church or who knows most about your church's process for bringing people into membership (this might be the senior pastor or someone else).

Encourage students to ask about your church's ideas on membership and belonging. Here are examples of questions:

- **What are the basic requisites to becoming a church member, if any?**

- **What is the process we follow to become members?**

- **In what ways, if any, are parents involved in our becoming members?**

Encourage your students to discover how they can more fully enter into the life of your church!

[SMALL GROUP DISCUSSION]

The Bottom Line

Use the following page of questions to have a small-group discussion about what's most important in the Christian faith. This could be done as one large group or in multiple groups of four or five people each.

handout on next page >>

ministryTOOLS

Breaking the Ice

1. If you had two minutes to talk on television about Jesus and you could say anything you wanted, what would you say? Rather than simply answering, act it out and have someone keep time.

2. How would you answer if someone asked you to describe Jesus?

Digging Deeper

3. Read John 14:5-7. What does this passage tell you about Jesus?

4. How does what Jesus said about himself differ from what you might have said about him on television or in response to someone's question about him?

5. These words of Jesus are both direct and speak of how he is exclusively unique. How do you feel about what Jesus said about himself?

Climbing Out

6. Discuss together:

☐ We sometimes think of Jesus as gentle, caring, and kind—and he was. But he was *also* direct and confrontational. Which side of Jesus' character seems most comfortable to you? Why?

☐ Why do you think having a full and accurate understanding of Jesus is a faith fundamental?

Degree in God Studies

You'll discover that your students are nearly always more interested in studying what they want to study than in what you want to teach.

Therein lies a challenge.

As a leader who cares about your students knowing Jesus, you'll want to connect students to experiences that fill in the faith fundamentals they need. They may decide that a lighter fare is tastier: games, movies, and activities.

Do this: Ask students to outline topics they want to explore. Then work with them to explore those topics from a biblical perspective, with an emphasis on introducing students to the living God. Providing solid biblical teaching in the context of a variety of topics won't be a stretch; God has a great deal to say about practically any subject.

Your role will be to coach the teenagers who are developing the topical studies (you didn't think *you'd* have to do everything, did you?) to capably consult Scripture and to present material that reflects a biblical perspective.

Announce that the topics to be studied will be your group's "Degree in God Studies." You've set the expectation that while the topical material might be varied, the goal will always be consistent: to better know and follow God.

Ask a student to design a diploma students will receive once they've completed the topical studies.

[CREATIVE RESEARCH]

Charting Churches

Do this activity to help your teenagers understand how churches and denominations are unique within the overall Christian church—and to see where your church fits into that picture. Beforehand, emphasize that this is *not* about what's right and wrong to believe or practice; this is about appreciating the richness of variety among Christians.

Have teenagers create a graph of various denominations. (Make sure that they understand this to be different denominations of *Christianity* and not other religions.) In the left-hand column, list various denominations students can think of, including your own denomination.

If your church does not belong to a specific affiliation, put the name of your church in one of the spaces in this column.

Across the top row, have students list the practices, doctrines, and ideas about which different denominations might have varied views. Suggest baptism, communion, church leadership, and worship style; your students will have additional suggestions.

Then invite teenagers to use the Internet or any reference books you provide to explore differences between denominations, including your own. Then ask these questions:

- **What can we learn by examining denominational differences?**
- **How is our church or denomination distinctive?**
- **Which—if any—of the differences are related to faith basics?**
- **How do you think differences should impact Christian friends from different churches?**

[FAITH EXPLORATION]

Creating a Creed

Using the Apostles' Creed as an example, discuss how Christians have clarified their understanding of faith basics throughout the ages.

SAY: **The Apostles' Creed was written sometime in the first few centuries of the church. It was called a "symbol" of the faith, meaning something that identified the faith or a way the faith was recognized.**

Early Christians included what they identified as the basics of the faith—their understanding of the fundamental truths of Christianity.

Distribute a copy of the Apostles' Creed handout to each student.

SAY: **Read through the handout with a pencil or pen in hand. As you read each line, decide if you believe what's written in the creed. If so, do nothing. If not, lightly cross off the part you don't believe. Take a few minutes to read through this ancient creed.**

After several minutes, continue.

SAY: **Now go back through the creed. If you crossed anything out, fill in what you *do* believe. In a few minutes, you'll discuss what you've changed with a partner.**

After several minutes, have students form pairs and discuss:

- **How is your creed like or unlike the Apostles' Creed?**
- **In what ways are you unsure about—or don't believe— what the Apostles' Creed accepts as faith basics?**
- **How open or closed are you to re-examining your personal creed?**

handout on next page >>

ministryTOOLS

The Apostles' Creed

I believe in God, the Father almighty,

　　creator of heaven and earth.

I believe in Jesus Christ, his only Son, our Lord.

　　He was conceived by the power of the

　　　　Holy Spirit and born of the Virgin Mary.

　　He suffered under Pontius Pilate,

　　　　was crucified, died, and was buried.

　　He descended to the dead.

　　On the third day **he rose again.**

　　He ascended into heaven, and is

　　　　seated at the right hand of the Father.

　　He will come again to judge

　　the living and the dead.

I believe in the Holy Spirit,

　　　　the holy catholic Church,

　　　the communion of saints,

　　　　the forgiveness of sins,

　　the resurrection of the body,

　　　　and the life everlasting.

Creating a Creed
(continued)

For a deeper discussion, ask students to look up the following Scripture references as they grapple with the Apostles' Creed:

I believe in God, the Father almighty, creator of heaven and earth.
(Genesis 1:1-3; Nehemiah 9:6; Psalm 86:10; 145:3; Acts 17:24-26; 1 Corinthians 8:6; Ephesians 4:6; Hebrews 11:3; Revelation 1:8)

I believe in Jesus Christ, his only Son, our Lord.
(John 10:30, 36-38; 1 Corinthians 8:6; Colossians 1:15, 17-19; 2:3, 9; 2 Peter 1:16-18)

He was conceived by the power of the Holy Spirit
(Matthew 1:18-25; Luke 2:8-11)

and born of the Virgin Mary.

He suffered under Pontius Pilate,

was crucified, died, and was buried.
(Isaiah 53:4-8; Matthew 27:57-60; Luke 23:13-25, 32-34, 44-46; 1 Corinthians 15:3-4)

He descended to the dead.
(Matthew 12:38-40; Acts 2:22-28; 1 Peter 3:18-19)

On the third day he rose again.
(Matthew 27:62-66; Luke 24:44-47; Romans 1:2-4; 1 Corinthians 15:12-14,19-20)

He ascended into heaven, and is seated at the right hand of the Father.
(Luke 24:49-51; John 20:17; Hebrews 1:1-3; 9:24; 10:12-13; 12:2)

He will come again to judge the living and the dead.
(Matthew 24:27, 36; 25:31-34, 41, 46; John 14:1-3; Acts 1:10-11; 1 Thessalonians 4:15-18; 2 Peter 3:10-13)

I believe in the Holy Spirit,
(John 14:16-18; Acts 1:8-9; 1 Corinthians 6:19-20; Galatians 5:22-23, 25; Ephesians 4:30-32)

the holy catholic Church,
(1 Corinthians 12:13-14, 27; Galatians 3:26-28; Ephesians 1:22-23; 2:18-22)

the communion of saints,
(Acts 2:42-47; 1 Corinthians 10:16-17; Galatians 6:2, 10; 1 John 1:5-7)

the forgiveness of sins,
(Matthew 26:26-28; Romans 5:6-10; 1 John 1:9; 2:1-2; 4:9-10)

the resurrection of the body,
(John 5:28-29; 6:39-40, 44; 1 Corinthians 15:23, 42-44, 50-54; Philippians 3:20-21)

and the life everlasting.
(John 3:14-16; 10:10; 11:25; 1 Peter 1:3-5; 1 John 5:11-13; Revelation 21:1, 3-4)

[FIELD TRIP]

Faith Field Trip

To strengthen teenagers' understanding of faith basics and common unity in the Christian faith, visit another church in your area that's different from your own church (have students contact the other church's staff and set up plans!).

Before the trip, ask your teenagers to make a list of things you'll look for, observe, and ask about at the church.

Tell your students that their mission is to find more *similarities* than differences between this church and your own.

After visiting the other church, create a gracious thank you note with all of your signatures, and send it to your hosts. Then debrief the experience together by discussing the following:

- **What stood out to you during our visit?**
- **What are the major similarities between our churches?**
- **What are the differences?**
- **Do you think the similarities or differences matter most, and why?**
- **What did you discover about the basics of the Christian faith?**

[DEVOTION]

To the Heart of Belief

Distribute this devotion to teenagers for them to do at home on their own time. The next time you meet, discuss what you experienced as you were doing the devotion.

handout on next page >>

Reflect . . .

What is the subject of your favorite song?

What do people usually write songs about?

Read Philippians 2:1-11.
(Verses 5-11 are thought
to be a hymn of the earliest Christians.)

Based on this song, what was closest to the
heart of the first Christians?

How is that like or unlike what you're focused on today?

If you didn't have to sing it for anyone, what would you write a song about?
Try creating a verse or two now.

Imagine the situations where one person actually writes or sings to someone else—like when people are dating or when someone honors a hero. Imagine what it would be like to sing directly to Jesus a song you had written. Can you do it now? **Go ahead...**

[ART IDEA]

The Artwork of God

Find a picture of the mosaic of Jesus in the south gallery of the Church of Hagia Sophia in modern-day Istanbul (originally Constantinople). You can find it in an art book or online (at www.iconofile.com/events/images/pantocrator_sophia.jpg or by searching "Hagia Sophia," "mosaic," and "pantocrator"). Show your group the book page, the printout, or the image on your computer screen.

ASK:

- **What do you think of this mosaic? What thoughts and feelings does it inspire in you?**

- **What do you think certain parts stand for? What about Jesus' hand? the colors? the letters?**

After a few suggestions, share these ideas from modern art scholars:

- **The circle with the cross behind his head is a halo, which stands for sanctity.**

- **The earthen-colored shirt and his hand giving a blessing represent the human side of Jesus, and the royal purple cloak and the Bible in his other hand represent the divine side of Jesus.**

- **The letters IC on the left-hand side are the Greek abbreviation of Jesus. The letters XC on the right are the Greek abbreviation of Christ.**

SAY: **The people who initially saw this were illiterate and couldn't read the Bible for themselves. So it was through art like this mosaic that they learned the basics of the Christian faith.**

ASK:

- **How can we explore the basics of faith?**
- **How might we help others learn the basics of the faith?**

BONUS IDEA: Art Hunt

Go with teenagers to an art museum, and discuss together what culture, literature, and art can reveal about faith in God. Have teenagers carry notepads and, in a kind of scavenger hunt, identify all of the spiritual symbols or connections they can find in the museum.

Before leaving the museum, invite teenagers to each sketch a piece of art that expresses their own beliefs and relationship with Jesus.

(SCAVENGER HUNT IDEA)

Photo faith

Have teenagers bring their own cameras, or have your group share one camera. If you have a large group, form small groups of about five people each, and give each group one camera.

Tell teenagers their mission is to go anywhere in the immediate area and take pictures of things that remind them of God.

Each person in the group needs to take at least one picture of something that connects to a truth about Jesus or faith. Teenagers might take pictures of nature, doorways, graveyards, and so on—the more innovative, the better!

Have everybody gather together after an hour. Display the pictures instantly if you're using digital cameras, or plan to get together next week if film needs to be developed.

Have students create a poster or PowerPoint slide show with pictures they took. Use this as a way to explore and discuss the truths of God and Christianity!

[AFFIRMATION IDEA]

The Bible Tells Me So

Give teenagers Bibles.

SAY: **Here's the thing about faith basics—they're not just for head knowledge. God expects us to *do* something with the truth revealed to us, and that usually translates into taking action.**

Have each teenager search the book of Matthew for one instruction from Jesus that applies to his or her life. For instance, Matthew 6:1-4 encourages Christ followers to not seek public acclaim for their "good deeds."

Encourage teenagers to form pairs and share the discoveries they found. Then have teenagers explain in their pairs how obeying Jesus (arguably a faith basic) looks in terms of the instructions they found.

Encourage teenagers to pray for each other, affirming each other in their roles as Christ followers.

[ASSESSMENT TOOL]

Faith Basics Survey

Photocopy the following form, and distribute it to each of your students. This questionnaire can give you insight into each teenager's faith and relationship with God. You may want to do this survey at the beginning of the school year so you can adapt your ministry strategy and activities to your students' specific needs.

handout on next page >>

ministryTOOLS

Faith Basics Survey

I would like to learn about (check all that apply)...

- ☐ eternal life
- ☐ a friendship with Jesus
- ☐ heaven
- ☐ the Holy Spirit
- ☐ God's qualities
- ☐ the Trinity
- ☐ the fruit of the Spirit
- ☐ the Bible
- ☐ the history of Christianity
- ☐ what this youth group is all about
- ☐ joy
- ☐ stress
- ☐ contentment
- ☐ love

- ☐ my true identity
- ☐ serving others
- ☐ doing well at school
- ☐ getting along with my family
- ☐ living faith in everyday ways
- ☐ making close friendships
- ☐ how to avoid sin
- ☐ what to do about guilt
- ☐ sharing my faith with others
- ☐ spiritual gifts
- ☐ how to pray
- ☐ how to study my Bible
- ☐ other: . . . .

Here are some questions I have about God or being a Christian:

I'd like to study these spiritual topics or books of the Bible:

Here are some needs I have that I'd like this youth group to help with:

Here are some suggestions for changes and improvements in the youth group at this church:

Chapter 2

EVERYDAY Faith

A Faith That Matters
by Rick Lawrence

The National Study of Youth and Religion offers the sharpest picture of teenagers' religious beliefs and behaviors that's ever been painted. And that picture portrays students' collective relationship with God as shallow at best.

While one out of every 10 or so adolescents has a living, vibrant, everyday relationship with God, nine out of 10 see God as a "Cosmic Therapist" or "Divine Butler" who exists only in the background of their lives, waiting to be summoned when they have a problem.

Through the centuries, followers of Christ not only experienced their relationship with Jesus as an everyday reality but often *gave up their lives* for the sake of his truth. For teenagers longing to give their lives to something meaningful, Jesus is truly the way, the truth, and the *life*. And an authentic, growing, intimate relationship with Jesus will overflow into everything teenagers do. Their faith will not be something they conjure up when they're desperate. It'll be something that really matters...and impacts their entire life.

Replacing the "Divine Butler" With an "Untamed Lion"

In C.S. Lewis' novel *The Lion, the Witch and the Wardrobe,* four English children are sent to a remote country village to live with a kindly professor in his big mansion. By accident, they enter an alternate world through a mysterious portal—a wardrobe—in the professor's home. Once in the magic land, called Narnia, they discover that the country is populated by talking animals and ruled by a vicious witch who keeps the seasons stuck on winter.

To avoid being captured by the witch, the children go to Mr. Beaver's home. He is a good and faithful Narnian who serves a great king—a lion named Aslan. Mr. Beaver tells the children that Aslan has returned to Narnia to make right everything the witch has destroyed. Mr. Beaver tells the children they will meet Aslan soon. One of the four, Lucy, asks if that's a safe thing to do, considering Aslan is a lion. Mr. Beaver says, " 'Course he isn't safe. But he's good. He's the King, I tell you."

In Narnia's Aslan, Lewis created a near-perfect metaphor for Christ. And he's as far from a "divine butler" as you can get.

Here is the great question of youth ministry: How do we move students from a mild affinity for Christ to an everyday relationship with him that matters—that informs all they say and do?

Not long ago, pollster George Gallup Jr. gave a broad update on the state of today's church. He said only one out of eight Americans has a "deep, transformative faith." That matches well with the results of the NSYR. And maybe that's why, according to Gallup, nine out of 10 churchgoing teenagers (88 percent) drop out of church by the time they graduate from college.

That's a sucker-punch statistic. It says most of our teenagers never cross the bridge from the land of window shoppers to the land of never-look-back Jesus followers. It says they're not connecting faith to the everyday things that make up their "real world." It says, basically, that God is irrelevant to their lives.

So is there hope for our ministries to teenagers? Absolutely. We must respond by doing what Jesus did—use the raw material of the prevailing culture to teach biblical truths.

When Jesus used fishing, farming, money, or common cultural practices to unveil his good news (bad news to some), he was bridging God's transcendent truths into the everyday world of the people. We must do the same.

Stop Retreating From the Real World

It's time to stop retreating from the "real world" into a Christian subculture that's becoming more and more fearful and non-welcoming. It's time to reassert our identity as people who live in the world but are not of it. It's time to focus on training young people to think critically about their cultural influences so they're well-armed to enter into the world without co-opting the world's system of thinking.

This is "in but not of" youth ministry.

Before we can enter into this fray, we have to be clear about what we're doing and why. Steve Turner's great book *Imagine: A Vision for Christians in the Arts* is a crucial primer. In it, Turner dissects what the Bible says about the "in but not of" life.

- **The Bible warns against "the world" and "worldliness."** God deemed the world he created "good." It remains "good." "Worldliness," on the other hand, is defined by Turner as the "rebellious system of thinking that's at war with the kingdom of heaven." Turner writes, "We become worldly not by engaging with the world but by allowing it to shape our thinking. Jesus prayed to God 'not that you take them out of the world but that you protect them from the evil one' (John 17:15)."

It's God's expressed desire that we stay right in the thick of the "world" while shrewdly, passionately countering its "rebellious system of thinking."

- **We can't love humans but hate human culture.** This is exactly why teenagers don't believe the church has much that's useful to say about their culture. Our "love" message seems two-faced. We say we love them but then say we hate the culture that often expresses and embraces their identity.

  Sadly, our students don't have many examples of "everyday" relationships with God that include sincere love for others and appreciation for their culture.

The Dichotomous Life We've Role Modeled

We have trained our students to look a lot like us: people who see no dissonance in living separate "everyday" and "church" lives, people whose primary focus is often to extract ourselves from culture, where salt and light have no impact.

The church has taught teenagers to respond to popular culture in three primary ways:

Denial and Blind Hope

Many in the church deal with the dissonance a threatening culture creates in them by denying that it could be impacting *their* students and assuming they'll be all right no matter what happens. The truth is that these adults are afraid of the truth and deal with it by denying reality.

We should be showing teenagers how to have the "veil removed" (2 Corinthians 3:18)—that means staring clear-eyed at the truth.

Retreat and Fortify

Another popular church response to a threatening culture is to raise imaginary walls in hopes of keeping the bad stuff out. That's why we've created Christian versions of…everything. But that's like building a corral under the surface of the sea. It looks like a corral, but it doesn't really keep anything out—or in, for that matter. Adults who want to retreat and fortify are acting out of fear.

We should be teaching teenagers how to act out of security, with strategies that are ultimately wise.

Attack, Attack, Attack

When all else fails, many in the church attack what seems threatening. However, this becomes a paradox—when you attack and try to destroy the cultural forces that teenagers use as mirrors, you guarantee a break in communication with those teenagers.

We should be maintaining communication with teenagers *so that* we can train them to think critically and biblically about their culture.

How Was Jesus Culturally Relevant?

Do we have real answers for teenagers, parents, and people in our congregations regarding pop culture? Most often, the answer is no. Yet we have a God-given and Christ-modeled responsibility to connect faith to real life.

Stop for a moment and think about the following examples of Jesus engaging his culture:

- He picked wheat on the Sabbath.
- He overturned the tables of the money-changers in the Temple.
- He allowed a known prostitute to crash his party and wash his feet with her tears and hair.
- He told people to give to Caesar what belongs to Caesar.
- He turned water into wine at the Cana wedding.

What are "now equivalents" for each example? What would Jesus have done in our current culture that's similar to what he did in ancient Jewish culture?

For example, a "now equivalent" of Jesus allowing a known prostitute to wash his feet with her tears and dry them with her hair might be Jesus inviting an avowed homosexual to go to a Sunday school class with him. These "now equivalents" might be offensive to some people in their churches, but the truth is that Jesus was *extremely* risky—and effective—in his approach to relevant ministry. How can we follow his example?

The dichotomous life we're living—our real-world self and our church self—has "trickled down" into our students' lives. We've taught them to live separate lives and adapt their core identity to their changing environments. We've effectively communicated to them that church is not a relevant place, a place where we can talk about the real world in critical and biblical ways.

Giving Our Students the Critical Tools They Need to Integrate Their Christian Faith Into Everyday Life

We need everyday ways to build biblical bridges from teenagers' cultural influences to God's truths. That's Jesus-style relevancy. You'll find powerful tools in the second part of this chapter, but here are a few suggestions to get your mental wheels turning.

Pay close attention to teenagers' entertainment.

Jesus was a subversive—he used the stuff of his surrounding culture to teach his followers about God, confounding his critics as he did. For example, people in Jesus' time entertained themselves at cultural celebrations. People in our time entertain themselves by watching films, listening to music, playing games (video and otherwise), and participating in recreational activities such as skateboarding, inline skating, and skiing.

Jesus used his people's favorite form of entertainment to teach about his true nature in John 2. You can use your students' favorite forms of entertainment to show them who Jesus really is, too.

Talk often about teenagers' media influences.

Group Magazine's survey found that just 17 percent of Christian teenagers say their participation in a church youth group has helped them "a lot" to think critically about films or videos (the numbers are 18 percent for non-Christian music, 12 percent for TV shows, 8 percent for video games, and 14 percent for Web sites).

Jesus often challenged the people of his day to think critically about the "givens" in their culture—for example, he challenged "acceptable" male-female contact when he engaged the woman at the well in John 4.

You can do the same by challenging students to come up with five things their favorite TV shows are teaching them. Then use what they come up with to target Bible study topics (making sure to use clips from their favorite shows as part of the studies).

Use what's cool in a teenager's world.

When the Apostle Paul noticed that the Greeks had a statue to an "Unknown God" in Athens, he used it as a portal to engage them with the gospel.

When we notice what's "cool" with teenagers, we can do what Paul did and use it to engage them with biblical truth. For example, challenge your group members to come up with a top-10 list of "things that are cool" that all the members agree on—they must whittle down their collective list until they have just 10 things on it. Then have them come up with a definition of what makes one thing cool and another thing not cool.

Use their list and definitions to filter topics into a Bible study series on "What Jesus Thinks Is Cool," using their examples throughout the study.

Give teenagers regular "problems" to solve.

Jesus used parables to introduce critical-thinking problems to his followers. We can do the same by giving students regular problems to solve.

Try breaking them down into three categories of "problem" questions: Gospel ("Why did Jesus treat the Gentile woman in Matthew 15 so harshly?"), cultural ("What makes music Christian?"), and relational ("What's the difference between our youth group and a clique?"). This will guide them to think about their lives and faith in ways they never have before.

Teach teenagers to question everything they take in.

Jesus often spurred people to question faulty cultural assumptions— typically, he started by saying, "You have heard it said…" We're aiming to train students to think critically instead of to passively take in the messages in their culture. It's just like reading the nutrition information on food products.

Help them analyze advertisements, commercials, TV shows, specific companies…you name it. Start with these questions: What's the message they want us to buy into? What's the promise they're offering? Is it a "Kingdom of God" promise?

You can use literally anything in popular culture to spur critical-thinking conversations with your teenagers. Soon, when they're driving alone in their cars, they'll hear something and a little voice inside will ask: Is that really true? When that happens, you've helped change the way they engage with their culture and opened up a new, deeply relevant phase in their relationship with God.

Use rites of passage to mark teenagers' important transitions.

Most non-Western cultures direct their young people through rites of passage that point them to adulthood. At the Jewish bar mitzvah service, 13-year-old boys are "recognized as adult Jews." And through the kisungu rite, Basanga girls of Zaire are initiated into the adult world through the symbolic death of their childhood.

But in Western society, we often ignore rites of passage. Young people desperately need adults who are wise enough to recognize the power of life transitions and embrace them with gospel-fueled experiences.

Rites of passage must include the following:

- **Separation**—Take your teenagers away from the familiar, and separate them from the props (music, friends, family, television, and so on) that define them. This could mean a retreat, a trip, or an unusual environment for an activity.

- **Transition**—Create activities that place students in limbo between their old faith status and their new one. They're not really "in" one or the other yet. Expect students to feel uncomfortable in this phase. Teenagers have a strong internal need to leave childhood behind and move into adulthood. But if the church doesn't provide them opportunities to do this, they'll find other, often more destructive, rites of passage.

- **Rebirth**—Return teenagers to the church or society, but now as more mature adult Christians. Traditions to confirm faith that involve the church body are good examples of the "rebirth" phase.

A legitimate rite of passage will spur younger teenagers to eagerly look forward to "their" day and older church members to treat "new initiates" more like peers than children.

Building Bridges

The whole point of Jesus' death and resurrection was to graft us back into God's family—to once again walk with him in the cool of the garden, as Adam and Eve did. God doesn't want "adherents" to a religion; he wants sons and daughters to enjoy him and be enjoyed by him. We can help teenagers live everyday relationships with God by building bridges between their real lives and God's mission, passion, and purpose.

You'll find some great bridge builders when you turn this page.

Affirmation, Affirmation, Affirmation

Affirming students is an essential part of helping them build a faith that matters. Just as parents should "catch their children" being good, take every opportunity you can to acknowledge students' efforts in their pursuit of God with affirmation statements, phone calls, e-mails, and notes.

Be intentional with statements such as "Ariana, thanks for sitting by Morgan her first night at youth group. It was cool that you didn't just sit with your comfortable set of friends but instead reached out to a newcomer." As much as you can, challenge students to live for God—and encourage even their baby steps. "I know it was a huge deal to only smoke one cigarette this weekend. Way to go, Jake."

We youth leaders should become "affirmation machines" to students, supporting and applauding when they live out kingdom principles and Bible truths in daily life.

Be specific in your affirmation. It's one thing to say, "Thanks for sitting with a poorly dressed visitor." It's another to say, "When you did that, I saw James 2:1-9 in action." Be intentional about helping students connect their actions to living out their Christian faith in daily life.

Sidewalk School

Block six consecutive Saturdays to go into low-income housing in your area and host Sidewalk School as a youth group. (You can choose another name that works better.)

From planning the "school" content to making the name tags to praying for all the children they'll interact with, have your students take full ownership of the event. This will help them put their faith into practice.

Each Saturday, escort your students as they knock on doors or distribute fliers, inviting all children—preschool through sixth grade—to come to Sidewalk School. Be clear that it will be similar to vacation Bible school. Then encourage your students to host the simple and fun program with games, a puppet show, interaction, a snack, a craft, and some songs. (Use Group Publishing's VBS program or FaithWeaver curriculum for this event!)

Remind your volunteers and students to enthusiastically sing along, play the games, and be involved in every activity.

No matter your students' own economic status, they will gain immeasurably from "giving themselves away" without a tangible reward. Make a big deal over them living out what the Bible says about helping the poor. Emphasize that doing so with an attitude of love, not pity, will help themselves and the kids they minister to feel rich.

Note: Because students are often unaware of what Scripture says about issues like serving the poor, debrief service sessions by sharing relevant Scripture passages and asking students how their actions are like or unlike what Scripture suggests.

In this case, ask students to read Matthew 25:31-45 and discuss:

- **In what ways are our attitudes like or unlike the attitudes expressed by the faithful in this parable?**

- **How can we live out our faith in serving others?**

[OUTREACH IDEA 2]

Letters of Encouragement

Have your students send notecards with words of encouragement and Bible verses to teenagers who are in juvenile detention (research and choose facilities that welcome this kind of mail).

Reaching out in this way will help your students put loving people as God does into practice. Help them find appropriate and sensitive passages of Scripture to include in their notes, and close note-writing sessions by debriefing the experience so teenagers connect their Christian faith with daily service.

[SMALL GROUP DISCUSSION]

Who Do I Know?

Here's a small-group discussion that will challenge your students not only in biblical thinking but also in biblical doing.

Anytime you provide something by which students can "take their faith" outside of church or small group, you help make their relationship with Jesus real and applicable. This kind of challenge gives your students applications, ideas, and challenges that can be fleshed out in practical ways at home, school, work, and in their relationships—both with friends and strangers.

Provide pens or pencils and copies of the "Who Do I Know?" (p. 54) hand-out for everyone.

Ask a volunteer to read Ephesians 3:7-11.

ASK: **According to verse 10, what is God's purpose?**

- **Before we talk about reaching others, what about you? What helps you be sure of your own faith?**

- **What makes Jesus "real" in your life?**

- **When you're not so sure of your faith, who do you talk to?**

- **Now what about your friends? What's your part in someone else's relationship with Jesus?**

SAY: **You won't always come out and directly help people grow in their relationships with Jesus. Sometimes you'll lead them to what the "next level" of faith is for them. They may not have even believed in God, but because of you, they may realize that God is real. Or maybe they don't go to church, but because of your kind and gentle persistence in reaching out to them, they decide to start coming to youth group with you.**

Have students take it from there with further examples of how they have strengthened or can strengthen others' faith.

ASK: **Who are people you don't get along with very well because of differences? Write their names down, but don't show anyone.**

After a few minutes, ASK:

- **What do these verses teach us about our role in these relationships?**

- **What's something you can do so that your faith impacts a friend's relationship with Jesus?**

As students share what they can do, challenge them to go beyond "pat" answers and be specific—for instance, praying for someone, leaving a note in a locker, inviting someone to church, taking someone to lunch, or helping someone with homework.

Have your students write down what they will do for the people they thought of.

SAY: **You've written down someone's name and what you will do as your part in that person's faith experience. Now pair off, and for just a few minutes, discuss this question with each other: How will praying for my friend and doing something for that person strengthen my own relationship with Jesus?**

After a couple of minutes or when there's a lull in the discussions,

SAY: **Now I want you to pray together for the people whose names you've written.**

After pairs have finished praying,

SAY: **You guys have to know how effective and cool it is that you're praying for each other's friends! Now I want you to commit to pray for the person whose name you wrote down and also to do what you said you would this week. Ask God for the boldness to follow through. Next week we'll share what we did and how it went.**

handout on next page >>

ministryTOOLS

Who Do I Know?

Who are people I don't get along with very well because of differences—
in background, culture, social status, interests, or another barrier?

Now consider . . .

What could my impact be on these people's faith?

What does God *want* me to do to strengthen their relationships with Jesus?

What Scriptures help me understand God's intent?

What *will* I do?

I commit to pray for _____
and do what God wants me to do this week.

Who Do I Know?

Who are people I don't get along with very well because of differences—
in background, culture, social status, interests, or another barrier?

Now consider . . .

What could my impact be on these people's faith?

What does God *want* me to do to strengthen their relationships with Jesus?

What Scriptures help me understand God's intent?

What *will* I do?

I commit to pray for_____
and do what God wants me to do this week.

[MISSION TRIP IDEA 1]

Adventure Journal

Help your students develop a passion for encouraging their own and others' Christian faith by going on mission trips—to places where students can serve people and experience God. During these trips, have students keep a journal of their experiences, feelings, perspectives, and relationship with God.

While students are outside their normal environment, encourage them to consider how the trip can teach them to serve others in their "regular" lives. Discuss how they can see their families, teachers, and friends in the same way they see these complete strangers—as people God loves and wants to become closer to.

Before a missions adventure, provide journals that include any Scripture verses appropriate for the trip's theme; a personal affirmation note from you; and enough pages for students to fill out one to two weeks prior to the trip, for the duration of the trip, and one to two weeks after you return. At the top of each page or for each day, provide specific headings that will guide students' journaling. Here are some suggestions:

- The Scripture I'm reflecting on is…

- My thoughts are…

- My prayer requests are…

- I thank God for…

- My expectations and goals for the trip are…

- I want God to use me to…

- I want this trip to affect my view of other people by…

continued on next page >>

Adventure Journal
(continued)

Include pages for students to fill out upon their return, using these suggestions:

- Some things that surprised me were…

- The main thing God did in me is…

- My view of others was affected…

- My perspective on Jesus changed…

- My perspective of myself and my life was impacted…

- My daily actions will change by…

[MISSION TRIP IDEA 2]

Adventure Debrief

After you return from a mission trip, host a debriefing meal to share pictures and talk about the experience. Ask a few volunteers to share portions of their journals that will encourage everyone else. Also distribute the "Trip Debrief" handout (p. 57), and ask students to write their answers to the questions and then give the handout to you. These answers will help students process their experience and give you valuable knowledge to apply to future mission and service trips.

handout on next page >>

Trip Debrief

1. What were your overall impressions of our trip, positive or negative?

2. What part did you play in our trip?

3. What did God show you about yourself and others?

4. What was frustrating for you, and how did you handle it?

5. What was most exciting or interesting for you? Why?

6. Describe your relationships with other group members during the trip, positive or negative.

7. Which part of the pre-trip training was most helpful?

8. Why would you want to be involved in another trip like this?

9. How did this trip change your life on a daily basis?

10. How can I be a better trip leader?

11. How did this experience affect your relationship with Jesus?

12. Do you see your faith in a new way? How so?

13. How can you better live out your faith every day?

Act It Out

On a dry-erase board, an overhead projector, or poster board, list current popular movies and TV shows that students call out.

Have students form groups of three or four that each focus on a specific movie or show.

Have each group act out a scene that demonstrates how one or more character's actions reveal the character's beliefs. For instance, if one character insults another, that may reveal anger or pride.

Also have students discuss which characters they relate to most and why.

- **What basic beliefs did these characters reveal through their interactions with one another?**

- **What are some of the themes of this show or movie?**

- **What are some of the messages this show or movie sends?**

- **What beliefs do your daily actions reveal to people around you?**

- **In what ways does this inspire you to make your faith matter more every day?**

Exploring Guys and Girls

Interacting with the opposite sex is an everyday occurrence in every teenager's life (even though some adults would prefer it wasn't!). Use this discussion opener to help students answer the question "How does God influence the way I think of and interact with others—particularly the opposite sex?"

Before a discussion on dating, purity, or friendship, separate the guys and girls. Have guys meet with male volunteer leaders and girls with female volunteers leaders, and have both groups discuss the same questions using the "Guys and Girls Discussion" handouts (pp. 60-61). This should only take about 10 to 15 minutes, depending on the size of your group.

Afterward, come back together, and have representatives from each group share what their group talked about. There will probably be some laughter, but that's OK! Stress that this is a time for both genders to learn about the opposite sex and help the opposite sex learn about them.

You may also have the two groups explore these Scripture passages together:

- 1 Timothy 5:2
- 1 Corinthians 6:19-20

BONUS IDEA

Take this idea a step further by having students read aloud statements that represent their genders' thoughts and values. For example, a girl might come up front and say, "I'm more than what you see on the outside. I may act a certain way at times because I'm insecure. But that doesn't mean I'm some stereotype. I want to be treated with respect and value." And a guy might say, "I may act a certain way around you, but that's just because I'm nervous and unsure. Remember that I have feelings, too, even though I may not easily show them."

It's powerful for guys and girls to hear others say what they wish the opposite sex would recognize about them.

handout on next page >>

ministryTOOLS

WHAT DO Guys THINK?

1. What do you think of the way girls dress, and why do you think they dress the way they do?

2. What do you think of the way girls act with each other, and why do you think they act the way they do?

3. What do you think of the way girls act around guys, and why do you think they act the way they do?

4. If there was one thing you wish girls knew about guys, what would it be?

5. How does your relationship with God influence the way you think about and interact with girls?

6. What can you do to help girls in their relationships with God?

WHAT DO Girls THINK?

1. What do you think of the way guys dress, and why do you think they dress the way they do?

2. What do you think of the way guys act with each other, and why do you think they act the way they do?

3. What do you think of the way guys act around girls, and why do you think they act the way they do?

4. If there was one thing you wish guys knew about girls, what would it be?

5. How does your relationship with God influence the way you think about and interact with guys?

6. What can you do to help guys in their relationships with God?

[GAME IDEA]

Keys to God's Heart

The Bible says that faith without works is dead, so we know God expects us to walk our talk. But the Bible also says that while man looks at the outward appearance, God looks at the heart. So which is more important—the outside or inside? Help teenagers navigate this question by leading a game that connects faith and life.

This is a great opportunity to involve a few of your artistic and creative students.

- On a large piece of poster board, make a simple path of squares, or use a simple board with a path on it from almost any board game.

- Use one die, and use game pieces or small keys, depending on the size of your group.

- Use the 22 instruction cards for this game (pp. 64-66), and make more on index cards if you'd like.

- Write "forward" or "backward" instructions on each card you make (examples on pages 64-66). Players move forward or backward on the game path.

- Have students draw a picture of a big heart on the end square of your game path. (This can be as simple as a childlike drawing with a goofy smiley face in the middle of the heart.)

- The game board doesn't need to be created on a computer— unless someone in your group would enjoy doing so. Feel free to keep the board fun and simple. Also, when you come up with your own game cards, use familiar places and "themes" from your community, such as "You were at Pamida buying those strong but effective breath strips when…" or "Old Mr. Handen, who we all know loves to recruit teenagers to help sell his produce in the parking lot of the hardware store on Saturdays, called you last minute to help this weekend—the one weekend you could go paintballing this month."

At the start of your time with teenagers, write this question on poster board or a dry-erase board: "If Jesus isn't a part of my everyday life, what's the point of following him?"

Throughout the following game and discussion, keep bringing students' attention back to this question. It's one of the deeply important questions behind this lighthearted game; the other question is "What are the keys to God's heart?" In other words, what really pleases God?

Emphasize to your group that this game is just for fun and to get them thinking about both their "action" and "heart" choices.

SAY: **Some of the instruction cards will have to do with everyday choices you make to do or not do certain things. But some of the cards will have to do with your thought life, motives, and heart attitudes. The point is that our relationships with Jesus are not just about what we do—lots of people do good things but don't have faith in God as a motivation.**

Neither is the Christian life just about what's in our hearts— many people really love God and *want* to serve him, but they make foolish choices and get stuck in sinful patterns that hurt themselves and others.

This adventure in knowing and loving God is about how we live on the outside and also about our personal relationship with God when we're not doing anything at all.

(If you aren't clear on these points, this game could send the wrong message that faith is about performance and that if teenagers don't get it right, they're blowing it with God.)

To de-emphasize the idea of someone winning and losing, simply encourage your students to "get the keys *to* God's heart as quickly as possible." The person who "gets" there first can opt to award bonus moves to other players who have drawn a negative card. For example, a student who "gets" to God's heart can say something like, "But you thought about it and decided to do the right thing." This will help your students encourage one another.

Here are a few examples for instruction cards. We encourage you to come up with more of your own. You can change the number of spaces a player moves as well. Have fun with this, laugh at yourself, encourage your students to do the same, and remind them once or twice that this is just to get them to think—not to make them paranoid about everything they think, say, and do.

If you want to use this game as a Bible study, add related Scriptures to some of the cards for students to look up.

instruction cards on next page >>

Keys to God's Heart
(continued)

INSTRUCTION CARDS

1 You heard one of your parents working outside. You knew that helping your parent would make life a little easier on him or her and that this practical way to honor your parent is a key to God's heart. So without being asked, you went out to help. Aren't you precious? Move ahead 2.

Related Scripture: Matthew 20:26-27

2 You heard one of your parents working outside, so you went downstairs and played on the computer…very quietly. Go back 2.

Related Scripture: Matthew 20:26-27

3 Your alarm went off, and you got up. Even though you were tired, you splashed water on your adorable face; then you spent time talking and listening to God and reading your Bible before you got ready for school. You put him first. Move ahead 3.

Related Scripture: Mark 1:35

4 Your alarm went off, and you hit the snooze button three times. Then you got up, rushed around getting ready for school, and hoped God wouldn't notice. He did. Go back 3.

Related Scripture: Mark 1:35

5 Your parent reminded you to do something you'd already done or were going to do. Even though it irritated you, you responded respectfully, assuring your parent that you'd already done or were about to do what you were asked. Then you (gasp) asked if you could do something else. Your parent fainted. Move ahead 2.

Related Scripture: Exodus 20:12

6 Your parent reminded you to do something you'd already done or were going to do. You didn't hide your irritation in your rolling eyes, clicking tongue, abrupt gasp, and voice tone when you barked back, "I KNOW ALREADY!!!" God may have just rolled his eyes, too. Go back 2.

Related Scripture: Exodus 20:12

7 Your least favorite teacher called on you to answer a question you're sure he knew you wouldn't know. Besides, you and your friends think this teacher doesn't like you and is part of a conspiracy to keep you in school until 2035. But knowing that submission to authority is a key to God's heart, you did your best to remember what little you knew about the topic and answered the question in a nice tone. You lived through it. Move ahead 1.

Related Scripture: Luke 6:40

8 Your least favorite teacher called on you to answer a question you're sure he knew you wouldn't know. You and your friends don't respect this teacher anyway, so your snotty response was no different from the teacher's condescending attitude toward you. But you forgot: God is looking at you, too.
Go back 1.

Related Scripture: Luke 6:40

9 You laughed at a degrading joke even though you knew it didn't please God, so you went back to the person who told it and said, "I thought it was funny, so I laughed, but when I thought about what it meant, I knew it was wrong. I'm not judging you, but I'm sorry I set a bad example by laughing at it." We all make mistakes, but you know that nothing's too small to deal with and a key to God's heart is admitting, learning from, and correcting your mistakes. Move ahead 3.

Related Scriptures: Proverbs 3:34; Ephesians 5:4

10 You laughed at a degrading joke even though you knew it didn't please God. You thought about going back and saying something to the person who told it, but the thought embarrassed you, so you shoved the idea out of your mind and moved on. God thinks you're better than that, even when you don't. He doesn't think anything's too small to deal with. Go back 3.

Related Scriptures: Proverbs 3:34, Ephesians 5:4

11 You struck up a conversation with a checkout clerk about some recent event in your community. As you were talking, the clerk gave you too much change. It was just enough to buy lunch at a drive-through, and you were in a hurry! First you thought, "Thank God for providing for me!" Then you remembered that personal integrity is a key to God's heart, so you handed the money back to the clerk, who looked at you like you had three heads and mumbled, "Thank you." God grinned at you. Move forward 2.

Related Scriptures: 1 Chronicles 29:17a; Psalm 25:21; Proverbs 10:9

12 You struck up a conversation with a checkout clerk about some recent event in your community. As you were talking, the clerk gave you too much change. It was just enough to buy lunch at a drive-through, and you were in a hurry! You thought, "Thank God for providing for me!" and hurried out the door. God loves you but is disappointed in your lack of integrity. He expects you to humble yourself, 'fess up to the clerk, and give the money back. In the meantime, go back 2.

Related Scriptures: 1 Chronicles 29:17a; Psalm 25:21; Proverbs 10:9

13 Your sibling talked down to you in front of your friends. You wished you could push a button and make the floor space underneath him or her open up. But you knew that treating others the way you want to be treated and not the way they treat you is a key to God's heart. So you ignored your sibling's remarks and quickly pointed out one of his or her great qualities. Your sibling was speechless, and God was smiling. Move forward 1.

Related Scripture: Matthew 7:12

14 Your sibling talked down to you in front of your friends. You wished you could push a button and make the floor space underneath him or her open up. You shot a smart-aleck remark right back and reminded your sibling of something that really embarrasses him or her. Touché! God loves you but would never say something like that to you. He expects you to apologize to your sibling and tell your friends that you shouldn't have said that. Go back 1.

Related Scripture: Matthew 7:12

continued on next page >>

ministryTOOLS

15 At the end of youth group the other night, you really thought about what the youth leader said and how to apply it to your life. You spent time alone on the steps of the stage or in a corner of the room just talking and listening to God. You might have even written down some thoughts he gave you. Move forward 3.

Related Scriptures: Jeremiah 29:13; James 1:25

16 At the end of youth group the other night, you really thought about what the youth leader said and how to apply it to your life. You considered praying about it, but it was too much mental work, you told yourself. Besides, what if God wanted you to actually *do* something about it? That would be even *more* work. You avoided God. He'll keep trying. Go back 3.

Related Scripture: James 1:22-25

17 You gave money anonymously to a missionary or needy friend just because you love God. You had other plans with your cash, but you know that giving out of compassion and obedience is a key to God's heart. Move forward 2.

Related Scripture: Matthew 10:42

18 You felt prompted by the Holy Spirit to give money to a missionary or needy friend. You had other plans with your cash, so you blew God off. He'll never blow you off. Go back 2.

Related Scripture: Matthew 10:42

19 You were online in a chat room when a guy you didn't know joined in and started talking trash, bragging about something he claimed to be great at. You thought the person was full of himself and might not even be who he said he was, but you responded tactfully. Then you asked him what he thought of God and hoped for a genuine conversation about faith. Because you wanted to represent God even in a chat room where no one except your friends knew you, you continued to talk like your real self. Move forward 1.

Related Scripture: Proverbs 10:23

20 You were online in a chat room when a guy you didn't know joined in and started talking trash, bragging about something he claimed to be great at. You thought the person was full of himself and might not even be who he said he was, but this was a chat room, after all, so you started acting like someone you're not and bragging about your own real or made-up achievements. Hey, it was kinda fun! God was left out of the conversation and your thoughts. Go back 1.

Related Scripture: Ephesians 4:29

21 A single mom in your neighborhood or church was moving one Saturday, and the youth pastor asked for students to show up that morning to help. You didn't have other plans, so you could have slept in. But you imagined yourself in her shoes and signed up to help. Move forward 2.

Related Scripture: Acts 20:35

22 A single mom in your neighborhood or church was moving one Saturday, and the youth pastor asked for students to show up that morning to help. You didn't have other plans. But it was your one morning to sleep in that week—no one was gonna rob you! Go back 2.

Related Scripture: Acts 20:35

ministryTOOLS

Graveyard vs. Construction

This activity and illustration are great to use with a group of new students who are transitioning into or out of your youth ministry or who are at the end of the school year. It's meant to get them to consider the "big picture" of their lives and to answer the question, "How am I going to live my life?"

You can simply have students experience the illustration and then discuss the suggested questions.

Or for greater impact, take your group to a cemetery, and go to the edge next to a road with something on the other side (such as apartments or businesses). The idea is that something from the "land of the living" is nearby. Obviously, you may have to tweak your wording and questions depending on the location of your cemetery. So the question might change to "Are you going to live your faith in the graveyard or in the town (or city)?" And your description of the area adjacent to the cemetery will fit the specifics.

If you don't want to actually go to a cemetery or if you want to keep the illustration as it was originally written, you could have students help you create the right atmosphere with cardboard tombstones and toy construction equipment. (Take it as far as you want with borrowed supplies from both funeral homes and local construction sites.)

Have students form small groups, and either have one student from each group read the following illustration aloud or have all group members read it together. Or you might gather as one group so one of your more dramatically inclined students can read this story aloud to everyone.

> On my way home the other day, I stopped at the cemetery. I looked for a secluded place to park. I noticed the big fenced-in construction site to my left. On this sunny day, I stopped on the road between the dismal, bland construction yard and the picturesque, tree-lined graveyard. I parked so that the construction site was on my left and the cemetery was on my right. I sat there quietly for a few minutes just looking, listening, and thinking.
>
> The construction area had several neatly aligned rows of cement pipes stacked on top of each other—some odd-shaped, but mostly round and big. There were piles of rocks and gravel here and there. I don't know much about construction, except that it always seems to take longer than it's supposed to.

continued on next page >>

Graveyard vs. Construction
(continued)

Anyway, I suppose it looked like any other construction site with building supplies and equipment. But to me, the rest of the location simply looked like a big yard of dirt, rocks, gravel, and broken concrete. The words hard *and* dangerous *came to mind. It definitely wasn't a place I'd let children play.*

God began stirring around simple truths in my heart as I compared the construction area with my left to the cemetery on my right. He reminded me that many people who follow him are "under construction" in some way or another. Being on the construction site usually means getting dirty. It often equates to long hours, sometimes in bad weather. Anyone who's ever worked in construction would say that it can be hard, exhausting, and, on occasion, dangerous work—you can even get hurt.

In life's construction yard, it could be that we've found ourselves fighting for stability in a frightening or tough situation. Perhaps we've been struggling with hidden sin, and we don't see freedom yet. Maybe we've been wrongly accused and find our character being tested. Or harder still, we've been justly accused of wrong and are facing intangible consequences we hadn't foreseen; at the same time, we're trying to regain intimacy and security with God and people. And some changes that we've asked for over and over have taken longer than we'd expected.

At one point I noticed a dump truck drive by and, a few minutes later, a maintenance truck. I sensed God say, "These are like my workers—the people who help others get through the building and repair process."

Then there was the cemetery, which was much more pleasing to the eye, despite what it represents. It was beautiful and serene-looking, with orderly rows of tombstones. Most of the headstones were decorated with pretty flowers and engraved with nice words. Eventually, the obvious occurred to me: The flowers were all fake, and those inscriptions meant nothing to the deceased. Is a cemetery a place to remember the past? At the right times, a comforting yes. Somewhere to reflect? Absolutely. For a few quiet moments alone, it's a nice place to visit...but thoroughly lifeless.

Just as I was sitting on the road between the construction yard and the graveyard, some people are in the road of decision: between continuing a long, sometimes painful, construction process or dwelling in a cemetery of regrets and forfeited dreams. Who, after a long-term battle of any kind, has never felt drained of faith or simply tired of fighting? Who, after struggling uphill with a certain issue, hasn't at some point feared that he or she would never see the "finished project" of mature character, healing, or restoration in his or her life? However, the Apostle Paul encourages us to remember that "We are pressed on every side by troubles, but we are not crushed. We are perplexed, but not driven to despair. We are hunted down, but never abandoned by God. We get knocked down, but we are not destroyed" (2 Corinthians 4:8-9).

When we are facing a change, whether self-imposed or life-imposed, we have a choice. We can remain in the graveyard. There we can exist (I purposely avoid the word "live") in a place that's quiet and undisturbed but where nothing's moving and it's thoroughly lifeless. Or we can opt to cross the road and go into the construction yard, where we can be fixed and rebuilt and can gain things we might not receive in any other place, where we can find ways to act on what God has taught us about living out our faith. It's dirty and dangerous. But that's where life is taking shape."

After this story is read, tell your students that it isn't meant to be morbid and that it isn't a discussion about death per se. The story is supposed to get them to consider the "big picture" of their lives and to answer the question, "How am I going to live my life—in the graveyard or in the construction yard?"

Have everyone stand and come to the road (or as close as they can between the cemetery and whatever is across from it).

SAY: **Take about five minutes to consider which side of the road you're on and which side of the road you *want* to be on. Talk to God, praying that he will strengthen your relationship with Jesus so that your faith becomes more and more real and impacts everything you do.**

After five minutes, gather back together, and give everyone a chance to share thoughts and feelings about the experience. Encourage complete honesty with the assurance that we're all in different places in our relationships with Jesus, so no one will judge harshly or look down on anyone.

continued on next page >>

Graveyard vs. Construction
(continued)

Here are a few suggested questions to help students process their thoughts:

- **Explain: Are you living out your faith in the construction yard or in the graveyard?**
- **Explain: Do you practice your faith in a way that's most comfortable for you, or do you feel challenged in some way to get out of your comfort zone?**
- **How do you want your faith to matter in the way you live?**
- **How can God help you?**
- **How can we encourage you?**

Pray together. Then, since this can be a deep and introspective activity, do something fun together (like get ice cream!).

[CREATIVE RESEARCH]

Rated "R" for Restricted

Nothing encourages students to make a true "I'll die for you" commitment like focusing on persecuted Christians around the world.

Together, take some time to explore stories about teenagers in countries that restrict Christianity. (Find out about underground churches using videos, books such as *Jesus Freaks*, or sites such as www.persecution.com.)

Have students discuss their thoughts and feelings. ASK:

- **What stood out to you most? Why?**
- **In what ways are persecuted Christians identified by their actions?**
- **If we were in a place of persecution, how would our actions in daily life identify us as Christ followers?**
- **How do persecuted Christians inspire you to make your faith matter in your everyday life?**

Have cards available for students to write down commitments to pray for persecuted Christians in restricted nations.

Go Where They Are

Few experiences can help students live out their faith more than serving at a homeless shelter. Plan with the shelter director to go on a Saturday and serve and interact with the people there. Depending on the types of programs available at the shelter, your group can serve by...

- serving meals.

- playing with children (or teaching them songs, games, and Scripture stories).

- cleaning and stocking shelves.

- donating personal things that are needed, such as clothes and bathroom items.

- performing skits, songs, or human videos.

- just asking questions and being great conversation partners!

After the experience, read Matthew 25:31-45 together and discuss the following:

- **In what ways are clients of homeless shelters "the least of these"?**

- **In what ways are we "the least of these"?**

- **In what ways did we minister to others today?**

- **In what ways did others minister to us?**

- **How did we live out our faith in Jesus today?**

[ROLE-PLAY IDEA]

God View

Explore with your students how they can look at the world and people through God's eyes. This can be a pretty intense topic, so have students do role-plays of various tough situations. This will help them investigate God's view of people and explore how their faith can impact everyday decisions. Here are a few situations to role-play:

- Your friend says her mom had an abortion before she had your friend. What do you say to your friend?
- The person you've been dating has been experimenting with substances you think might be dangerous. What do you do?
- One of your best friends has been visiting gay Web sites and tells you in confidence about an attraction for the same sex. What do you say?
- Your friend seems depressed and confesses that she's thinking about cutting herself. What do you say?
- Someone at school says very harsh, rude things to you—particularly targeting your faith. What's your response?

After students have done the role-plays, discuss how their actions and words reflected—or didn't reflect—God's view of people. ASK:

- **In what ways does God expect his followers to interact with others?**
- **How did Jesus interact with others? Share examples from the Bible.**
- **What were Jesus' purposes when he interacted with people?**
- **How can we mirror Jesus' purposes in our daily lives?**

Faith Invasion

Think back to yesterday. What did you do, how much time did you spend doing it, and how did it reflect your relationship with Jesus? How did your faith really matter from moment to moment? To figure out how you're living your faith in everyday ways—and to discover how your relationship with Jesus can have an even greater impact in every moment—fill in the blanks below. Then go through the questions on these two pages.

Phone Calls:
Time:_____minutes/hours (circle one)
How my faith mattered:

Sports/Extracurriculars:
Time:_____minutes/hours (circle one)
How my faith mattered:

Friendships:
Time:_____minutes/hours (circle one)
How my faith mattered:

Hobbies/Interests:
Time: _____ minutes/hours (circle one)
How my faith mattered:

Internet:
Time:_____minutes/hours (circle one)
How my faith mattered:

Prayer/Scripture:
Time:_____minutes/hours (circle one)
How my faith mattered:

Family Activity:
Time:_____minutes/hours (circle one)
How my faith mattered:

Volunteering/Service:
Time:_____minutes/hours (circle one)
How my faith mattered:

School/Homework:
Time:_____ minutes/hours (circle one)
How my faith mattered:

Bible Study/Small Group:
Time:_____minutes/hours (circle one)
How my faith mattered:

Job/Chores:
Time:_____ minutes/hours (circle one)
How my faith mattered:

Youth Group/Church:
Time:_____minutes/hours (circle one)
How my faith mattered:

handout continued on next page >>

Faith Invasion ...continued

TV/Movies:

Time:_____ minutes/hours (circle one)
How my faith mattered:

Video Games:

Time:_____ minutes/hours (circle one)
How my faith mattered:

Music:

Time:_____minutes/hours (circle one)
How my faith mattered:

Other:

Time:_____. minutes/hours (circle one)
How my faith mattered:

Magazines/Books:

Time: _____minutes/hours (circle one)
How my faith mattered:

● What, if anything, surprised you about what you did? What surprised you about the time you spent doing it?

● In what areas of life does your faith really matter?

● In what areas should your faith matter more?

● What are your thoughts and feelings about the time you spent with God yesterday?

● In what ways can your relationship with Jesus be reflected in every area of your life?

● What commitment will you make to develop an "everyday" faith that impacts all your time?

● Write a brief prayer to God now, asking that he will draw you closer to him and help you live your faith so it impacts every second of every day.

Suggested Resources

Here are some resources to help your students build an everyday faith:

- *Essential Messages for Youth Ministry* (Group Publishing)
- *Incredible Illustrations: News You Can Use in Your Ministry* (Group Publishing)
- *Holy Wow: Boost Your Youth Ministry Creativity* (Group Publishing)
- *Grace-Based Youth Ministry,* Chris Hill (Group Publishing)
- *The Seven Checkpoints: Seven Principles Every Teenager Needs to Know,* Andy Stanley and Stuart Hall
- *Vision Moments: Creating Lasting Truths in the Lives of Your Students,* Bo Boshers and Keith Cote

Suggested Web Sites

- www.youthministry.com
- www.ministryandmedia.com (Ministry and Media)
- www.groupworkcamps.com (Group Workcamps Foundation)
- www.compassion.com (Compassion International)

Student Resource Shelf

Stock one or two shelves of resources students can borrow. Include small-group resources, devotions, and interactive Bible studies for them to do with their friends or small groups.

Supplying students with resources will encourage them in their relationships with Jesus and help make their faith really matter.

Here are some suggestions of Group resources to make available:

- *Friendzee: Christian Character*
- *Living the Beatitudes of Jesus: 30 Devotional Experiences*
- *Tasting the Fruit of the Spirit: 30 Devotional Experiences*

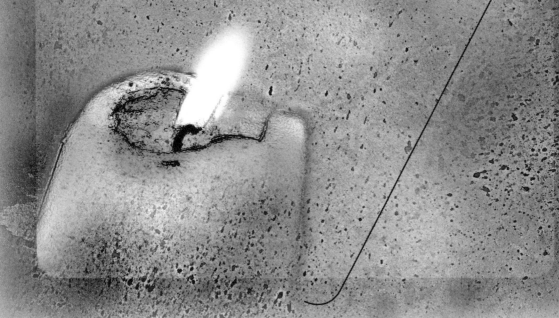

Chapter 3

Faith
EXPRESSED

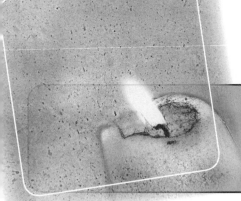

God Talk
by Rick Lawrence

One of the more sobering results from the National Study of Youth and Religion is that the overwhelming majority of teenagers in the United States are "incredibly inarticulate" about what they believe and how their beliefs impact their everyday lives.

Christian teenagers may believe in God and have committed their lives to follow Jesus, but they have a very hard time giving a coherent explanation for any of it. More unsettling is that most of them can't explain the connection between their Christian faith and their everyday life experiences. Churches and parents don't seem to be training young people to understand and express their faith anymore, which is something that was a clear priority in the past.

The good news is that we can do something about that…starting today.

Telling God's Story

A couple of years ago, Leo, a swashbuckling businessman who'd pursued professional and personal adventures his whole life, died instantly when the airplane he was piloting slammed into the side of a Colorado mountain. Leo had made and lost his fortune several times over, climbed 14,000-foot peaks on the sunset side of his 70s, and piloted his own Cessna for more than 25 years.

In so many ways, Leo was an unusual man—he loved to talk about faith in God and frequently pursued religious conversations with people he'd just met, but he claimed he was a staunch atheist. He was a man full of passionate opinions on politics, social issues, economics, and world history. This man was an overshadowing force in the lives of those who knew him—the kind of man who leaves a wake of impact behind him, who lived his life with such vigor that death seemed an impossibility.

At an informal memorial gathering, Leo's family and friends assembled to honor him with speeches, stories, and poems. The last person to speak was a young man who seemed somehow out of place in the lineup. He said, "I met Leo when I was 18—I think that was the best age to meet him, when I was young. A few minutes after I was first introduced to him, he looked me square in the eye and asked, 'What do you stand for?' I didn't even know I was supposed to be thinking of questions like that. But that question has dominated my life ever since."

It's a stunning question. Who could have stared back into Leo's steely eyes and answered well? And what would happen if you asked your teenagers Leo's question?

Would they have a hint?

Would they subvert the question with humor or feigned ignorance or "the right answer"?

Would they stammer or disappoint you with an underwhelming answer?

Or would their answers bring tears to your eyes?

Today's teenagers don't know how to express what they believe. The question is this: Are they truly ignorant of their religious beliefs, or have they simply not learned how to talk about the Christian faith in a natural way? Most likely, it's a combination of both.

Leo's question gets at the core of the problem. Our teenagers need a clearer picture of what a relationship with Jesus is all about, and they need ways to practice telling the Great Story—that is, how God's story and their story have merged to become one story.

"What do you stand for?" could be the bookend question for your ministry. It could be one of the first questions your teenagers hear when they enter your ministry and the last thing they hear before they leave your ministry for career or college. The difference between their answers—coming and going—is all about what you, in partnership with their parents, do to help them know Christ and make him known.

So how can we help teenagers express their faith to others? How can we help them describe what it's like to be in a personal relationship with Jesus?

Entering the De-Compartmentalized Zone

When Brother Lawrence wrote the classic book *The Practice of the Presence of God*, he was a dishwasher in a 17th-century monastery. The book chronicles his efforts to turn his everyday life into a perpetual prayer to God.

Do you teach or model a spiritual life characterized by an ongoing conversation or by compartmentalized times when you connect? In court, a transcriptionist records every spoken word for the record. How would your interior transcripts read? How infused with God conversations would they be?

Teach teenagers to practice the presence by inviting God into their everyday living. That's far more important than spectacular but infrequent "God moments."

Martyred Columbine student Cassie Bernall kicked off a worldwide "let's get serious" movement among young people with one little word: *yes*. Definitely a spectacular God moment.

Trouble is, the girl who was hiding next to Cassie under a library desk says the exchange between Bernall and Dylan Klebold never happened. Police investigators think students in the library likely heard another student, not Cassie, answer yes to a gunman's question about her belief in God.

So what difference does it make? It would be great if the answer were "none." Unfortunately, it does make a difference to many people—if doubt is cast on Cassie's last act of faith, the spiritual impact of her life diminishes in their eyes. That's not just sad; it's typical of the magnetic pull grandiose actions have on us and how easily we ignore the courage it takes a Christian teenager to commit to an everyday relationship with God.

And Cassie's story of courage has little to do with what happened in the Columbine library.

Long before April 20, 1999, Cassie made countless courageous—but uncelebrated—decisions to express and defend her tender faith in God. In the book *She Said Yes,* Misty Bernall describes how her daughter, over and over, reaffirmed her faith by tiny heroic acts. Cassie's friend Cassandra recounts a conversation she had with her a few months before the rampage: "She said to me, 'You know, I don't even feel God anymore. God seems so far away. I'm going to keep pushing on, but it's really hard right now; I just don't feel him anymore.' "

Grandiose statements of our faith are so seldom required of Christian teenagers that they hardly warrant attention. But everyday statements, the "pushing on" kind that are seldom seen, are a precious treasure. You can help your teenagers express their faith in God every day by training them to do things such as...

- praying when they'd rather do or say something else. Better yet, they can ask a friend to pray with them.

- saying no to something they know isn't God-honoring and then explaining why. For example, "No, that would hurt the most important relationship in my life—my relationship with Jesus."

- listening well to a friend's problem and then answering with an example of how God has dealt with the same or similar issue in their own life.

- asking forgiveness of those they hurt, instead of simply offering an apology. (And teach them to say "I forgive you" when others apologize.) This opens up an opportunity to tell people about God's forgiveness.

- paying more attention to God's claims on their lives than to their claims on God (in other words, thinking and talking more about what God might want them to do than what they want God to do for *them*).

- speaking up in defense of Jesus when others (including teachers) want to write him off.

Underlying all these ideas is a foundation of expressing faith in Christ—a lost emphasis and art for today's Christian teenagers. It's time to reclaim it.

Training to Talk About Faith

If we truly believe that today's Christian teenagers are "untrained" in their ability to express what they believe, then we need to come up with a training plan.

Here are four ideas for getting started on that training plan.

Use a neutral third party to give teenagers opportunities to discuss Christian beliefs.

Neutral third parties are attention-getters that spark conversation but shift the focus away from you. For example, you can use a book study to raise tough questions about faith in Christ, and then you and your teenagers can verbally wrestle with the answers together. This will get teenagers in the habit of talking about a relationship with God and answering the more difficult questions about faith.

Or invite a guest or panel of guests who are knowledgeable about the Bible to answer your teenagers' questions about Jesus, the Bible, what it means to live out a Christian faith, and so on. Collect the questions in advance, but also allow for spontaneous follow-up questions. Listening to others talk about faith will help your students better learn how to articulate their own beliefs.

Or invite several Christian college students to list the challenges to their faith they've experienced since leaving high school. Use these challenges as an exploration of how teenagers will continue living out and expressing their faith in future years.

Come up with a "Christian faith basics plan" so teenagers will know how to explain the foundation of their beliefs.

If you're going to train your teenagers to express their faith well, what's the "ammo" they're going to need? Use the great tools from chapter 1!

And when you explore the basics of the Christian faith, include the following:

- an overview of the major religious perspectives
- information about creation and evolution
- evidence for the deity of Christ
- evidence for the Resurrection
- the validity and reliability of the Bible
- a healthy dose of teaching about the purpose of apologetics—to reach out with the wonderful news about a relationship with Jesus, not to win arguments or bludgeon people with truth

Encourage teenagers to be prepared with answers that reflect God's truths.

This is as simple as giving teenagers a set of questions and having them carefully build answers that express their belief in God and the truths of Christian faith. This will equip them for the inevitable "questioning" times by friends, peers, teammates, teachers…or pretty much anyone they'll interact with throughout their lives. Because they're prepared, they'll stand firm and ready to give thoughtful, God-led responses. Here are some suggested questions to start with:

- How do I know that God exists?
- Who is Jesus?
- What does it mean that the Bible is God's Word?
- Why do I believe that the Bible is true?
- How does someone get to heaven?
- What does it mean to be a Christian?
- What is sin?
- What are the differences between Christianity and other religions?

Teach teenagers that the best way to express faith is by a transformed life.

Help your students understand that while it's important to practice telling people about Christianity, that's not even close to the only way—or the most vivid way—of expressing their faith in God. The single most powerful expression of their relationship with Jesus is how they *live*. When the grace, joy, and utter transformation that God brings overflow naturally into their entire lives, everyone around them will sit up and take notice, because they're articulating their faith in ways they couldn't even plan.

Reveal the Real Jesus

Here's an important reminder at the tail end of a "what you can do" list. I know from almost two decades of asking teenagers and adults about their faith trajectories that what Jesus Christ modeled is always more impactful than what Jesus Christ talked about. Teenagers say they're most powerfully influenced when other Christians reveal a spontaneous Christ-like attitude in the context of relationship.

The bottom line: In relationship, teenagers are impacted for eternity by "the real you." Is "the real you" a grace-living, God-loving, raised-from-the-dead Christian? If so, the "accidental" things you do are impacting your teenagers for Christ as much as your planned activities.

Great activities help teenagers learn how to express an authentic relationship with Christ—and you'll find some really great activities in the pages that follow.

Personal Stories of Faith

It's important to give students opportunities to practice sharing about their relationships with Jesus. Here's one way to do that.

First, have a volunteer read aloud 1 Thessalonians 2:8: "We loved you so much that we shared with you not only God's Good News but our own lives, too."

Then have students form groups of three. Ask one student in each group to share his or her Christian faith story.

(If non-Christian students are involved in this, you might make it clear that this faith story *doesn't* have to be about a mature or longtime relationship with Jesus; students can talk about any thoughts on faith they have, even if they don't consider themselves Christians.)

You might give some cues for the Christian faith stories by helping students think through these questions:

- **How has my family influenced my view of faith and God?**
- **How would I describe my thoughts about Jesus?**
- **What are some of the themes that have been part of my faith journey?**
- **In what moments have I felt closest to God?**
- **When have I felt farthest from God?**
- **What has impacted or strengthened my faith?**

Have the other two students in each group listen and ask good follow-up questions; then have each of them take a turn. By the end, all students will have practiced putting their thoughts on faith and God into words—and they'll be that much more prepared to do it again. Discuss together:

continued on next page >>

Personal Stories of faith
(continued)

- **What was it like to express your personal story of faith?**
- **What's easy about articulating our Christian faith? What's tough?**
- **What was valuable about having two other people listen to you?**
- **How can you clearly express your Christian faith to people in your life?**

BONUS IDEA

You also might set this up as a student-led training time, where each of the three people has a specific mission during the activity. For instance, while one student talks, another should be the listener and question-asker. The third student should be an observer whose job it is to give feedback (by letting the speaker know if he or she is clear and by saying things such as "You really connected with me when you said…").

Have students do five minutes of sharing and five minutes of feedback. Then have everyone switch roles.

At the end, have students discuss the questions at the top of this page plus these:

- **What is it like to get feedback about the way you expressed your faith?**
- **How can your friends' encouragement and input help you talk about your relationship with God?**

[OUTREACH EVENT]

Can You Hear Me?

As they become people who regularly express their faith in Jesus, your students should make a habit of really understanding and caring about the people they're talking to. Use this activity to help them grow a genuine interest in others' views and opinions.

Hold a night where students invite their non-Christian or unchurched friends. Students should tell their friends that the goal for the evening is for students to listen to their friends. (Make sure they know this isn't a back-handed way of "preaching" at them.)

Let your teenagers' parents know about this night ahead of time, and explain that you want your teenagers to better understand their peers' perspectives and assumptions about Christianity.

Encourage your students to ask questions that will help them understand their friends' views on the Christian faith—this will lead your students to new sensitivity and wisdom when they share about their relationship with Jesus.

Here are some questions to include:

- **What's your impression—positive or negative—of Christians?**
- **What's the hardest thing for you to accept about Christianity?**
- **What's the best thing to you about Christianity?**
- **When you hear "Jesus," what's your first reaction? Why?**
- **What faith alternative, if any, seems better for you? Why?**
- **How do you personally approach the idea of faith and spirituality?**

Encourage your students to listen carefully and respectfully and to respond honestly and appropriately—but urge them not to argue. The point of this experience isn't to debate the truth of Christianity. Instead, it is to see more clearly that the starting point of articulating our faith lies in truly seeking to understand others' most authentic perspectives.

Afterward, thank your visitors, and then spend some time hanging out together (pizza's always a good idea). Be sure to debrief the night with the group. ASK:

- **What did you learn from your friends?**
- **What surprised you? didn't surprise you?**
- **How are you encouraged to be a better listener? more caring?**
- **How will getting a better understanding of your friends' views on Christianity help you express your faith?**

ministryTOOLS

"Here I Am" Collage

Have students express their faith without words through personal collages. Provide magazines, newspapers, and art supplies so each student can create a collage of what he or she stands for spiritually. Here are the questions each person should answer through the collage:

- At the core of my being, who am I?
- What does my relationship with God look like?
- What pictures and images best describe my faith?
- What are my spiritual beliefs?
- How do I feel about Jesus?
- What do I hope for?

Afterward, have each student take two minutes to share his or her collage. Thank everyone for sharing. ASK:

- **How did you express your faith through your collage?**

- **How does articulating your faith like this help you grow closer to God?**

Take the collages, and put them up on the youth group wall. Ask the group to discuss what these collages all have in common. Some of the ideas you come up with might include joy, unconditional love, freedom, truth, or security. ASK:

- **How might we reflect these parts of our Christian faith through everything we do?**

- **What are other creative ways you can express your faith and who you are spiritually?**

[DEVOTION 1]

First Things First

Teach students the importance of the Shema (the Great Commandment). Help them to understand that of all the far-reaching things Jesus taught about and modeled, it all came down to the Shema: Love God (Deuteronomy 6:4-9). And there's no better expression of the Christian faith than living this out.

You might want to tell students that in Jesus' day, reciting the Shema was frequent (even over the course of a day), and it was about renewing one's relationship with God and accepting God's ultimate reign—again and again and again.

Together, read Deuteronomy 6:4-5 and Matthew 22:34-39. Then have students form pairs and discuss these questions:

- **Why do you think the Shema is so important to having a relationship with Jesus?**
- **How will the Shema impact your life and Christian faith?**
- **In what ways are you living out the Shema? not living it out?**
- **How can you express love for God by loving others?**
- **How can the Shema lead you to express your faith to others?**

Make a commitment together to memorize the Shema and recite it when each of you wakes up in the morning. You may also recite it together whenever you meet as a group.

ministryTOOLS

Beatitudinal

Jesus gave some of his most powerful teaching in the Sermon on the Mount (Matthew 5) and especially in the introductory verses of the sermon, which are often called the Beatitudes. These provide powerful insight into how your students might live their Christian faith boldly, clearly, and compassionately.

Have your students form small groups for this devotion. Have each group work together to paraphrase the "upside down" values taught in the Sermon on the Mount. Each group should choose a few values and translate them into a language that relates to their 21st-century lives. They should also provide examples of those values.

After students have translated the Beatitudes into what Jesus might say to them today, have groups read their translations aloud.

Then discuss these questions together:

- **What kind of impact would living out your beatitude have on others?**
- **How might living out your beatitude express faith in Jesus?**
- **What makes living this beatitude tough?**
- **Why is this beatitude important to God?**

Have students pray together to end the devotion. Encourage students to commit to putting these beatitudes—both the "originals" and the ones they created—into practice every day. This will be a vivid and powerful way to express their faith in Jesus.

Senior Legacy

To give your teenagers the opportunity to express their faith and encourage others in faith, have them interact in a unique and possibly challenging way.

For a certain number of weeks, have the seniors plan and lead all the Bible studies, large-group meetings, outreach events, small groups, devotion times, and so on. Basically, they will be responsible for guiding the younger teenagers through exploring Christian faith and talking about a relationship with Jesus.

Here are some additional suggestions as seniors take ownership of the youth group times:

- Have seniors lead in pairs to share the load and for mutual encouragement.
- Suggest that seniors choose an adult volunteer to be their "helper" and advocate.
- Remind seniors to set schedules to make sure any planning, preparation, and setup is done in plenty of time.
- Have seniors make video "ads" promoting what the group will be exploring and doing.

While the older teenagers are leading the youth group times, be an available resource and advisor, but do not step in and take over. Pray for all the students, and observe closely how things go—especially paying attention to the discussions and "breakthroughs" students of all ages have as they interact.

After the set amount of time is over, process the experience with both sets of students.

With the seniors, discuss these questions:

- **What was this experience like?**
- **How did you grow in your relationship with God?**
- **In what ways did you articulate your Christian faith to others?**
- **How did you help others articulate their faith?**
- **How did this strengthen your commitment to express your relationship with Jesus to others?**

continued on next page >>

ministryTOOLS

Senior Legacy (continued)

With the younger students, discuss these questions:

- **What was this experience like?**
- **How did you grow in your relationship with God?**
- **In what ways did you express your Christian faith to others?**
- **How did others help you learn how to share about your relationship with Jesus?**
- **How did this strengthen your commitment to express your relationship with Jesus to others?**

Use this experience to build in your group an atmosphere of teamwork, student leadership, and especially openness about faith.

[FIELD TRIP]

Following Jesus from Here to There

To help your students see how they can live out a faith in Jesus that others will notice, go to different places where your students spend time (school, home, the stadium, a coffee shop, the mall, a computer desk, and so on). At each place, talk about what it means to follow Jesus there.

Push students beyond the superficial responses like praying before the track meet or meeting for Bible study at the local coffee shop. Ask deep questions that get them considering how they are expressing their faith everywhere— even without using words.

Try these questions as a starting point:

- **What's it like to be here?**
- **Who do you interact with while you're here?**
- **What makes it hardest to live out your relationship with Jesus in this place?**
- **What, if anything, happens here that helps you express your faith in Jesus?**
- **How will you better reflect your relationship with Jesus while you're here?**

At each location, pray together that your students' faith in Jesus will overflow in powerful ways and impact others.

Duct-Tape Gospel

Help your students practice "speaking the gospel" without words.

Set up four stations around the room that each represent an area of life where teenagers can share the gospel with others:

- station 1—family
- station 2—school
- station 3—city
- station 4—church

At each station, have items, pictures, or words that describe the specific area. For example, at the family station, you may set out a playhouse or dollhouse, a picture of a family, the word "divorce" written on paper or a puzzle piece, a model car, and a telephone.

Also set markers and a blank sheet of paper at each station.

When students arrive, give each of them a piece of duct tape. (Test this out beforehand; if you'd prefer, you may also use another kind of tape.)

SAY: **Lightly put the duct tape on your mouth, making sure it's not going to be painful to rip off. From now on, talking isn't allowed. St. Francis of Assisi is believed to have said, "Preach the Gospel at all times and when necessary use words." For the next bit of time, we're going to explore what it means to express our faith without using words.**

Indicate the four stations around the room.

SAY: **You'll go to each station, sit down, and think about what it means for you to share the gospel without talking in that area of your life. Basically, besides *verbally* telling people how Jesus died on the cross so they could be in a personal relationship with him, how could you express that awesome truth?**

Before leaving each station, use a marker to express at least one idea you have. But, again, you don't have to use words—you can draw a symbol or a picture or just write letters that represent your idea.

You can visit the stations in any order you'd like. Begin.

Allow enough time for each student to visit all the stations. Then have students *gently* take the duct tape off their mouths and sit in a circle. Collect the piece of paper with ideas from each station, and set the paper in the center of your circle.

continued on next page >>

ministryTOOLS

Duct-Tape Gospel (continued)

Discuss the experience using these questions as a guide:

- **What was this like for you?**
- **What ideas did you come up with for sharing faith in Jesus without using words?**
- **What makes this difficult?**
- **When might it be most meaningful to use words?**
- **How will you commit to sharing the gospel in each of these areas?**

Encourage each student to leave with one concrete way he or she will express faith in Jesus without using words.

[PRAYER IDEA]

A Little BIG Prayer

As students come into the room, have ambient music playing that creates a reflective, God-centered atmosphere.

Give each participant paper, a pencil, and a copy of the prayer traditionally attributed to St. Francis of Assisi (p. 93). Let students know they shouldn't move or write—just reflect on what this prayer means.

Now give students some brief background: St. Francis of Assisi, born in 1181 or 1182, was a devoted monk who dedicated himself to charity and to the sharing of the gospel.

Or you might want to assign the background to a couple of your students; have them see what they can find out about St. Francis and come prepared to share it with the group.

In unison, read the prayer slowly, deliberately, and out loud.

SAY: **Now we'll journal our thoughts about this prayer. Try rewriting it in your own language so it's more personal and perhaps clearer to you.**

As you move into the journaling part of the activity, you might want to change the music to something lighter and more lively.

After students have finished journaling, discuss these questions:

- **What stands out to you most in this prayer?**
- **How are you encouraged to live out your faith in Jesus?**
- **What effect will living out your faith have on others?**

handout on next page >>

ministryTOOLS

St. Francis of Assisi

Lord, make me an instrument of your peace.

Where there is hatred, let me bring **love**.

Where there is injury, let me bring **pardon**.

Where there is discord, let me bring **union**.

Where there is doubt, let me bring **faith**.

Where there is error, let me bring **truth**.

Where there is despair, let me bring **hope**.

Where there is sadness, let me bring **joy**.

Where there is darkness, let me bring **light**.

O Divine Master,

grant that I may not so much **seek**

to be consoled as to **console**,

to be understood as to **understand**,

to be loved as to **love**.

For it is in giving that we **receive**.

It is in pardoning that we are **pardoned**.

It is in dying that we are

born to eternal life.

Quiet Service

Involve your students in compassionate service as a way of expressing Jesus' love and grace. Try this idea:

Together, find out some needs of people in the community (or teenagers at your students' schools), and have everybody in your group bring at least one needed and newly purchased item (such as food, books, clothing, small appliances, and so on).

Gather together in small groups, and have each group choose about three or four addresses.

Have each group travel to their addresses and quietly leave the items on the doorsteps of the homes. If you think people are home, set the gift down, ring the doorbell, and leave quietly. Don't leave a note or in any way indicate who you are. Gather together and pray for each of these people, asking that God would pour his love and grace on them and meet their needs. Pray also that each of you would express Jesus' love to others in the ways God wants you to.

Discuss with your students the power of quiet acts of kindness and compassion—the kind that aren't broadcast or bragged about.

ASK:

- **What's it like to do something kind or compassionate without the person knowing about it?**
- **How does helping to meet people's needs reflect Jesus' love and grace?**
- **How might serving and praying for others affect their relationships with Jesus?**
- **How else can you express your faith through "secret service"?**

Have a volunteer read Matthew 6:3-4 aloud: "But when you give to someone in need, don't let your left hand know what your right hand is doing. Give your gifts in private, and your Father, who sees everything, will reward you."

- **What does it mean to not let your left hand know what your right hand is doing?**
- **How can you share your faith in Jesus through kindness— without expecting any thanks?**

Pray together that God will use your quiet gifts of kindness.

faith Translation

Help students discover ways they can express their faith by asking them to create a Christian Translation Guide. Have students form pairs or trios, and ask groups to each make a list of words or phrases they hear Christians use a lot—or that are commonly used in church—that non-Christians may not understand. Encourage students to think of friends who may not know anything about the Bible or a relationship with Jesus and to include words and phrases those friends wouldn't connect with.

Then have groups write "translations"—words or phrases that explain the ideas in language that is clear to a non-Christian. Let students know that the goal is to use language their friends would understand and connect with, but the translation shouldn't weaken any underlying meaning and truth.

After about five minutes, ask groups to share the original words and the translations they came up with.

Have one or two volunteers read Acts 17:16-34. ASK:

- **What was the first thing Paul referred to as he began speaking?**
- **What kind of language did Paul use? Why is this important?**
- **Why do you think Paul quoted a Greek poet while preaching the gospel?**
- **How can you compare our activity to Paul's approach?**
- **How might using specific language and words help you share your faith more effectively?**
- **How will you use Paul's approach and the ideas from these lists to tell others about your faith in Jesus?**

ministryTOOLS

Outside Messages

Teenagers' sense of self-worth and identity is often inaccurate, due to the emotional and physical turmoil they're experiencing. But the cultural images and messages they're bombarded with daily can even further damage their fragile beliefs about who they are—as people and as God's children.

To get students into the habit of processing cultural messages, begin a discussion using popular magazines. Gather magazines that your students are familiar with and that will provide opportunity for discussion about identity and self-worth. (Use your judgment concerning which magazines are relevant and acceptable to the discussion.)

Have youth form small groups of only girls and only guys. Ask group members to glance through the magazines and discuss what they observe. After a few minutes, gather together for a discussion.

ASK:

- **What messages are being sent to you through the images and articles in these magazines?**
- **What do these magazines expect you to believe about yourself?**
- **How does this line up with what God thinks about you? what the Bible says about you?**
- **What misperceptions can you find? What truths?**
- **How does looking through the magazine make you feel about yourself? your life?**

SAY: **Let's read aloud some absolutely true messages. Here are some things that God wants you to know about yourself.**

Here are some suggested Scripture passages to read aloud together:

- John 15:12-16
- Romans 5:6-11
- 2 Corinthians 5:14-15
- Psalm 139
- Ephesians 2:4
- John 4:10
- Romans 12:4-8
- 1 Peter 1:10-11

End by praying together. Ask that God would help each of you understand the truth of who you are—and live by God's messages, not any other.

Suggested Resources

Here are some resources to encourage your students to understand and express their faith:

- *Transformation Stations: Committing My Relationships to God* (Group Publishing)
- *Walking in His Footsteps: A Multimedia Journey Through Jesus' Last Week* (Group Publishing)
- *Creative Faith Ah-Ha's!* Thom and Joani Schultz (Group Publishing)
- *Faith Metaphors: 50 Interactive Object Lessons for Youth Ministry* (Group Publishing)
- *Book of Common Prayer*
- *Jesus With Dirty Feet: A Down-To-Earth Look at Christianity for the Curious & Skeptical*, Don Everts
- *Journey to Jesus*, Robert E. Webber

Chapter 4

SPIRITUAL Training

Training Teenagers for Spiritual Growth
by Rick Lawrence

Even though half of all U.S. teenagers say religion is important to them, National Study of Youth and Religion researchers found that the majority practice their faith "sporadically or not at all." Just four out of 10 pray every day, belong to a youth group, and attend religious services every week or more often.

So belief in God and a respect for "spirituality" are strong among young people, but relatively few are living their faith in practical, everyday ways. They're going to need more training in faith practices than they're currently getting—from both their parents and their youth leaders—to make that leap.

Train as Jesus Did

You can learn a lot about youth ministry from toddlers. According to brain researchers, it's like the Fourth of July inside their little heads. At two points in our lives, we experience explosive brain growth over a relatively short period of time—one is while we're toddlers and the other happens during...you guessed it, middle school/junior high.

Talk about fireworks. Researchers have discovered that very little children and young teenagers are standing on the same developmental cliff's edge—namely, they don't yet have the brainpower to make good decisions. It turns out they're missing the "mental traffic cop" that helps most adults sort and compare information before reacting to something. That means knee-jerk reactions drive most young teenagers. And they often incorrectly label others' emotions.

Until the last decade, neuroscientists thought the human brain was fully developed by puberty. Using magnetic resonance imaging technology, they now know that's not true. "The teenage brain is a work in progress," says neuroscientist Sandra Witelson in a U.S. News & World Report interview. Surprise, surprise.

But here's why this is important. Teenagers need training if they're going to learn anything—from driving a car to learning to type to living their Christian faith.

Not long ago, I was discussing the results of the NSYR with lead researcher Christian Smith, and he told me he was amazed at how few adolescents have had spiritual training of any kind. That runs directly counter to the way Jesus trained his disciples in the things of God. He knew they'd have to be taught to follow him—he didn't assume they'd just pick it up by hanging out with him.

How Jesus Trained

Looking for ways to implement spiritual training into your ministry mind-set? Here are some ideas:

- Let's say a guy in your group asks you about heaven. "What do I have to do to get there?" he asks. So you tell him to sell his nice car; give up his scholarship to the Ivy League university; give away all the money he's carefully saved; go to a remote, poverty-stricken place; and serve the poor in Jesus' name— then ask you the same question when he returns. Jesus did something like that with the rich young ruler (Luke 18:18-27).

- Some gay teenagers from your church or area start an after-school support group. So you ask if you can hang out with them (maybe serve as an adult adviser?). You eat meals; go out and get coffee; and basically spend some authentic, quality time together. Jesus did something like that with the woman at the well (John 4:1-26).

- You ask your students what one question they'll ask God when they see him face to face. The most popular question is "Does hell really exist?" But instead of answering the question directly, you tell them a story about what happens to bread when you leave it sitting on the kitchen counter for a few days. Jesus did something like that with his disciples in Matthew 13.

Jesus, of course, was a fantastic spiritual trainer. And we believe he had the ability to impact people this way because, well...he's God. It seems utter nonsense—or worse, impractical—for us to follow his example.

A lot of youth leaders believe that a preached message is the best way to train teenagers; they just don't think active and interactive experiences are practical in real life. But Jesus proved, through these interactions and many more, that not only are active and interactive experiences practical but they're also amazingly effective.

We shouldn't be expected to teach the way Jesus taught. In fact, Jesus expects us to be better teachers and spiritual trainers than he was. Remember his words in John 14:12: "I tell you the truth, anyone who believes in me will do the same works I have done, and even greater works, because I am going to be with the Father."

It's Not as Hard as We Make It

Jesus said we'd teach greater lessons than he did, but we typically don't. Why not? Maybe we youth leaders make it harder than it needs to be. Jesus took risks when he trained his followers because he cared more about long-term learning than short-term results. We can do that, too.

Let's focus on five Jesus-style training strategies.

Spiritually train teenagers using parables.

A parable is a compelling story with a hook. It has a beginning, middle, and end. But it doesn't force-feed its meaning to listeners. Different people will learn different things from the same parable. Jesus used parables to help his followers understand what God and his kingdom were like. (In fact, many of Jesus' parables began with him saying, "The Kingdom of Heaven is like...")

For example, in the story of the prodigal son, Jesus portrayed God as an intimate, passionate, pursuing father—a radical characterization for the Jews of his day. But at the end of the parable, you're left wondering what will happen to both the older and younger sons. Clearly, the father in the story is good, but that might not keep the older son from resenting the grace offered to his brother.

Of course, any biblical parable is worth retelling. But God didn't stop speaking in parables when the canon of Scripture was closed. Our contemporary culture is full of stories that communicate God's true personality and character—you can find them in films, popular music, books, and even news stories.

I think film is one of the most important tools in youth ministry. Even bad films have short segments that make for great biblical parables. Show the clip, and then debrief using great questions that are tied to a Bible passage.

If that's a little too risky for your church environment, then challenge your students to take a Bible parable and translate it into a contemporary setting with contemporary characters. Then debrief using follow-up questions designed to get at the "truth nugget" in the story.

Parables throw out a truth wrapped in a story and leave it for the listeners to do what they will. That's risky in teaching teenagers because some teenagers might not get it.

But some will. And for them, that personal discovery will impact their lives long after the youth meeting has ended. You could fill an entire year of training times by focusing on Jesus' parables alone.

Spiritually train teenagers by modeling.

If your life were a book, what would the plot teach those who were reading you? Who would the protagonist be in your story? Who'd be the enemy? What would others say was motivating the main character (you)? At the heart of modeling is a desire to make your life a story worth telling.

Spiritual training by modeling is simply acting in a way that teaches. It means living purposefully, and it means looking for opportunities to demonstrate your words.

Try studying and imitating Jesus-style modeling with your teenagers. For example, Jesus was always praying (see an example in Luke 5:15-16). We don't know what he prayed about much of the time, how he expressed his prayers, or how God responded to him. But we do know he talked to God constantly, typically alone, and sometimes all night.

His disciples noticed this. The result? In Luke 11:1, one of Jesus' disciples said, "Lord, teach us to pray." Wouldn't you love for your students to request that? Well, Jesus did it without ever saying a word. And you're doing it right now in your ministry.

Spiritually train teenagers by asking good questions.

CNN's Larry King once gave an interview that revealed his question-asking secrets. Check them out—they'll remind you of Jesus. And they'll give you ideas on how to lead students into meaningful spiritual training using just a simple question.

- **Be curious.**

- **Follow through.** Another way to say this is to be *passionately present.*

- **Focus.** Think of yourself as a detective trying to unravel a mystery—and the mystery is the person in front of you.

- **Avoid "yes" and "no" questions.** Keep questions open ended, and urge follow-up answers with "Why?" and "Explain more."

- **Don't fake it.** This gets at a myth of youth ministry: Teenagers expect us to be cool if we hope to develop a relationship with them. But that's wrong. Be yourself—that's how they'll trust you.

- **Get them in your shoes.** Another way of saying this is that when you're pursuing teenagers with tough questions, don't forget to be honest about your own story.

These skills for asking questions can be learned. How? Practice. Challenge yourself to be the best question-asker in your church. In every encounter with a teenager, ask at least one great question. And, lo and behold, you'll become a Jesus-style spiritual trainer.

Spiritually train teenagers by giving them ownership—and letting them make mistakes.

We all know that failure is a master teacher, but we still seem hard-wired to rescue teenagers from the consequences of their decisions and actions.

However, when we shield students from making mistakes, we also shield them from meaningful responsibility and valuable learning opportunities.

If you expect students to be active in helping plan your ministry activities, you'll give them a rash of opportunities to make mistakes that teach. They'll make fewer mistakes if they're only passive consumers of your ministry—but they'll also learn a lot less.

When we give students ownership over their own experiences, we train them the way Jesus trained his followers when he sent them out in pairs to preach his gospel.

Take a hard look at the number and kind of decisions you're making in your ministry, and then brainstorm how you can give half of them away to your teenagers for the sake of their spiritual training.

Spiritually train teenagers using strategies that are R.E.A.L.

Years ago Group's leaders, Thom and Joani Schultz, created an acronym to describe the way Jesus taught—R.E.A.L. We've broken it down for you below. After reading about it, what R.E.A.L. ways can you think of to guide teenagers into spiritual training that'll help them live out what they believe?

- **R stands for relational.** This means that when teenagers interact with you and with each other, they radically deepen their learning as they build Christian friendships. God could have chosen any method to train us in his ways, but he sent his Son, Jesus, because God is passionately relational. He sent us a person to be in a relationship with, not a set of principles to apply.

- **E is for experiential.** Effective youth leaders know that experiences are the best teachers. Teenagers will remember biblical truths up to nine times longer when they're based on experiences than when they're simply heard or read. Think about the spiritual discipline of faith. When Jesus wanted to teach about faith, he plunged his disciples into faith-focused experiences: Peter stepping out of the boat, the feeding of the 5,000...we could go on and on.

- **A means applicable.** The aim of youth ministry is to equip young people to be both hearers and doers of God's Word—and that means always building bridges between spiritual truths and teenagers' real world. Again, this is why Jesus used Roman coins, cultural traditions, farming, fishing, and other everyday activities as the context for most of his teachings.

- **L stands for learner-based.** Since people learn in different ways, they understand and retain more biblical truths when the learning process takes into consideration how they learn best. When you train teenagers using a learner-based filter, you don't pronounce them "trained" until they prove it. Most of us think our job is done when we've taught, but the truth is, our job is done when our students prove they've learned.

What's Your Real Goal?

At the end of his earthly life, Jesus summed up his ministry goal in a prayer: "I have revealed you to the ones you gave me from this world. They were always yours. You gave them to me, and they have kept your word. Now they know that everything I have is a gift from you" (John 17:6-7).

As youth leaders, we can adopt that prayer for our students and for our ministries. It's possible to help teenagers spiritually train just as Jesus helped the people he ministered to...if we humble ourselves and heed God's words to the Apostle Paul: "My grace is all you need. My power works best in weakness" (2 Corinthians 12:9). If we risk for the sake of lifelong learning, we'll feel out of control sometimes—weak and unsure. When we do, we open a portal to God's power to impact our students.

There's no better time to start risking more than...right now. Turn the page for a host of ideas that'll get you going.

ministryTOOLS

[by Steve Argue & Dave Livermore]

Maybe Monks

Fourth- and fifth-century monks practiced the art of *lectio divina,* which means "divine reading." It's a way of digesting God's Word as one digests food, and it emphasizes reading, meditation, prayer, and contemplation of the Word of God. Use lectio divina to help your students practice Scripture "training" so that God's Word will sink into their hearts and flow out through their everyday lives.

BASIC PROCESS

First read a Scripture passage three times slowly. Then encourage students to ask any questions they have about the passage. Next, seek to understand the Scripture through resources such as multiple translations, commentaries, or Bible dictionaries. Then begin to memorize the passage together.

Here's an example of how you can practice lectio divina with your teenagers.

Distribute the "Lectio Divina" handout (p. 106) to students, and then read Psalm 62:5-7 three times slowly: "Let all that I am wait quietly before God, for my hope is in him. He alone is my rock and my salvation, my fortress where I will not be shaken. My victory and honor come from God alone. He is my refuge, a rock where no enemy can reach me."

After the third reading, walk through each of the handout steps together, allowing students to guide the experience so it's personally meaningful to each of them.

Afterward, discuss these questions:

- **How did this experience make you feel? What did it make you think about?**
- **How did exploring Scripture in this way draw you close to God?**
- **Why might you continue to study God's Word in this same way?**
- **How can you intentionally dig into the Bible and live out God's truths in your everyday life?**

handout on next page >>

Meditation

As Psalm 62:5-7 is read three times, begin to let specific phrases sink in.
Let God speak to you as you consider:

"God alone,"   "My hope is in him,"   "He is my refuge,"

and "_____."

Ponder these phrases; reflect on what they mean.

Prayer

Let the Scripture passage move you to respond to
God by praying to him. In the space below, write a
response to God about how he spoke to you
through his Word.

Now let others in on your conversation with God.
Form groups of two to four, and read your prayers
to one another.

Contemplation

Continue to reflect on God's Word, and commit to memorizing this passage
(start now!).

Consider what the Holy Spirit has shown you through this passage.

Think about how you can put it into practice in your life, and write down your
thoughts. Begin with…

the necessity of solitude

the necessity of community

(HOLIDAY IDEA)

Mark Your Calendar

With your students, explore the meaning behind each part of the Christian calendar: Advent, Christmas, Epiphany, Lent, Easter, and Pentecost. This will equip them to understand the great significance of holidays that are often celebrated by people only in secular ways. It will also lead them to practice their faith through Christ-centered spiritual traditions.

You might use books or helpful Web sites to gather thorough information. As you begin the tradition of engaging in holidays as a group, have students plan and take ownership of the events.

Here are two flexible frameworks to use in your ministry:

Getting Ready for Easter (Lent)

If Easter is the ultimate climax in the Christian calendar, how do we prepare ourselves for it? We've got some ideas that the church has passed along for many, many years.

Tell students that Lent emphasizes our desperate need for Christ's sacrifice. Here are some things you might incorporate into your Lenten experience:

- Begin on Ash Wednesday by having a candlelit ceremony to signal the inauguration of Lent. Remind your group that Ash Wednesday focuses on our vulnerability ("from ashes we have come; to ashes we will return").

  Allow a lot of time for reflection, repentance, and committing the next 6½ weeks to collectively anticipating Easter.

- Highlight the following three disciplines of Lent, and find ways to practice them:

  - fasting from things that falsely replace your dependence on God
  - praying
  - giving to those in need

continued on next page >>

ministryTOOLS

Mark Your Calendar
[continued]

- Discuss students' thoughts and feelings during your celebration of Lent, using these questions as a guide.

ASK:

- **What is God showing you as you participate in the celebration of Lent?**
- **What is hard about this experience?**
- **What's exciting about it?**
- **What have you learned about yourself? others? God?**
- **How can you continue to intentionally celebrate the meaning of this time?**
- **How will this sort of spiritual training lead you closer to Jesus?**

Getting Ready for Christmas (Advent)

What if, instead of counting shopping days until Christmas, we anticipate Christmas the way the church has for hundreds of years? Here are some ideas and resources:

- Offer a specific Scripture reading schedule for the Advent season.
- Decide to forego the Christmas tree in the youth room for a year, and build the biggest Advent wreath you can. Make it the central focus of your gatherings for the next several weeks.
- Talk with your senior pastor about how your youth group might be involved in the Advent season through readings, prayer, artistic expression, and so on.
- Discuss students' thoughts and feelings during your celebration of Advent, using these questions as a guide.

ASK:

- **What is God showing you as you participate in the celebration of Advent?**
- **What is most meaningful to you about this experience?**
- **What have you learned about God?**
- **How can you continue to intentionally celebrate the meaning of this time?**
- **How will this sort of spiritual training lead you closer to Jesus?**

[BIBLE STUDY]

Reading the Lines—
and In-Between the Lines

Encourage students to read through the Bible so they can begin to understand the overall story of God and what faith in Jesus is all about. Give them tools for this important spiritual training.

For instance, give your group a schedule to read through the Bible in a year. While people can start out strong, it's common to fade or get so behind that giving up is tempting. So tell students upfront that you know they can accomplish it, and encourage them often to persevere in sticking to the schedule.

Each week, you also might provide a devotional that is based on a Bible passage (maybe based on the passage you taught in class, youth group, or small group). Ask students to spend time reflecting on the passage throughout the week. Give them some questions that push them to understand the Bible on a deeper, more personal level.

ASK:

- **What has it been like for you to read through the Bible?**

- **How does committing to explore the Bible impact your relationship with Jesus?**

- **In what ways is this good and healthy "spiritual training" for you?**

Getting It Write

Two important experiences in spiritual training are prayers and sharing prayers with others. Use this idea to help students grow stronger relationships with God and others.

Set out markers and pens, hang large sheets of white paper all around the room, and declare that tonight is a night of worship—but without singing (though you might choose to have music playing in the background).

Guide students through a time of worshipping God—focusing on praise, repentance, and requests—and have them spend time writing their prayers on the wall. Let students know they can express their worship any way they'd like using words, symbols, or pictures. Emphasize that others will be reading what they write, so they shouldn't use specific names.

Tell students to also take time to look at what others are praying. Students may stop and pray with others, silently or aloud, as they record their prayers together.

Afterward, discuss these questions together:

- **What was this prayer and worship time like for you?**
- **In what ways does expressing your prayers bring you closer to God?**
- **Why it is important to share our prayers with each other?**
- **In your spiritual life, how can you write prayers and share prayers with others more often?**

Leave the prayers up, and encourage teenagers to come back to this area once in the next week to read, reflect on, and pray about what your group wrote.

[PRAYER IDEA 2]

The Follower's Prayer

Use this idea to help students understand and experience Jesus' prayer in Matthew 6 and begin to use it as a "root" prayer in their lives that they'll return to again and again.

Distribute the "Follower's Prayer" handout (pp. 112-113) to each student. Together, read it aloud slowly and deliberately. Then give everyone time to pray individually.

Encourage students to circle or underline the words or phrases that best express their own prayers.

After everyone has finished, close in prayer together. ASK:

- **What parts of this prayer most clearly expressed your heart and thoughts? Explain.**
- **What was it like for you to communicate with God like this?**
- **How will returning to this prayer again and again strengthen your relationship with God?**

BONUS IDEAS

You may also…

- have students paraphrase this prayer on their own or paraphrase it together as a group.
- look at each section separately over the course of a few weeks, exploring it together and searching for Scripture passages that connect.
- memorize the prayer together.
- end each of your times together by reciting this prayer, letting it take on special meaning for your group.

handout on next page >>

ministryTOOLS

Heavenly father

Father...Abba...Daddy. I take comfort in knowing that you are my Father, a Father who is intimately concerned and connected to his children—to me, to my closest friends, to my youth group. Heavenly Father, I look at the world from my little corner. But you look at the world from heaven. You know everything. You can do anything. Nothing escapes your sight, your attention, your reach...yesterday, tomorrow, today.

Hallowed be your name...

I praise your name—the I AM. It is sacred, holy, unique, and glorious. May my thoughts and words reflect your holiness and sacredness so people see you clearly in my life and in our church. When I think of you, may I pause in wonder...awe...fear.

Your kingdom come...

May your reign come today, and may I believe that it is coming more today than yesterday. I want you to be king. Jesus, you said, "The Kingdom of God is near." I believe that because you, the King, came near. May you draw near in my life today, great King. Change me as you have promised to do. May my gathering with other people in my youth group and church be a tangible expression of you. And may we, your body, come to the hurting, the needy, the most desperate and forsaken places—to the poor, the broken, and the powerless. May your kingdom come to the friends I so desperately love—to their homes, schools, workplaces, and hangouts. May it come to the people who feel like losers. May it come to our neighborhoods.

Your will be done, on earth as it is in heaven.

Bend my will toward yours. May I seek to know your will and your timing. May I trust you to do your work in my life, my world, and the world that you so passionately love. May we not see your world as a lost cause but seek to bring heaven back to earth because of what you did on the cross.

Please provide the food we need.

My prayer is a declaration of dependence. I need you today, tomorrow, and every day for the things that seem impossible and even for the things I feel I have under control. May I discover your continual provision and realize personally that in you, Jesus, all things are held together. I may never measure up to the standards and expectations of teachers, my so-called friends, my parents, and my co-workers, but you sustain me.

Forgive and make me forgiving.

Heavenly Father, forgive me for my sin. I hate that word *sin*. I would rather call it a mistake or lack of judgment. But it's sin—rebellion, treason, and hatred toward you. Have mercy on me based on your righteousness, Jesus. Thank you for speaking in my defense (1 John 2:1). And as I experience your mercy and grace, may I pass on the same to others who have wronged me.

Lead me, deliver me...

...away from the things that tempt me—money, impurity, popularity, selfishness, acceptance, approval, success. Help me deal with the realities of life and the pitfalls that await me apart from your leading. May my times with you be times of clinging to you, declaring that I need to be led lest I perish.

Ultimately, I have hope for...
Yours is the kingdom,
Yours is the power,
Yours is the glory
forever and ever.

And may I never take the prayer you gave me, Jesus—the follower's prayer—lightly.

Amen.

So be it. May it be true. Right on.

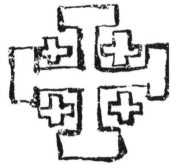

[SERVICE IDEA 1]

Generating Generosity

Generous giving as a reflection of Jesus' love is an essential part of teenagers' spiritual training. Together, find ways to give generously, tangibly, and cheerfully. Choose a project where students will give out of what they have and will also become involved with people beyond just sending money.

Here are some ideas:

- **Annual "Liberate Your Closet" Day—** Encourage students to empty their closets of everything they don't wear anymore (or—a better challenge—of things they do wear!). Pile up the clothes and take them to a local shelter together.

- **Empty Pockets Night—**Would your students be willing to give whatever is in their pockets for people who have nothing in their pockets?

- **Skip a Meal Deal—**Encourage students to skip lunch every Friday for one month; then give the money to a ministry or organization of their choice.

- **30 Hour Famine—** World Vision does a great job of offering an event that helps students identify with the poor and hungry and then do something about it. Together, check out the 30 Hour Famine information (www.30hourfamine.org) and consider how you'll be involved. Talk as a group about how to make this more than just a 30-hour experience and something that becomes a value for you throughout the year.

After the experience, discuss these questions:

- **How difficult or easy is it for you to give generously? Why?**
- **Why should giving be a frequent thing in a Christian's life?**
- **How does giving generously to others reflect Jesus' love?**
- **How can you train yourself to reflect Jesus' love every day?**

[SERVICE IDEA 2]

Get the Message?

Help students train themselves to identify—and respond to—messages that tell them something other than what God tells them.

Try this: Divide the room in half by vertically draping a large sheet over a clothesline, string, or cord. You may also hang a piece of newsprint. On one side of the sheet or newsprint, have a screen and an overhead projection unit, and set out snacks and refreshments. On the other side of the sheet, have pens and markers or paint and brushes available.

Stand near the sheet or newsprint, on the opposite side from the overhead.

Ask students to talk about the messages they "hear" every day from the world around them—any messages that hurt them, bring them down, discourage them, or get in the way of hearing what God might want to say to them. Have students take turns writing these on the sheet or newsprint. ASK:

- **How do these messages prevent us from seeing what's true about God and ourselves?**
- **How do we help each other get beyond these distracting messages?**

Now have students work together to take the sheet or newsprint down. Turn on the projector, and have a few overhead markers ready.

Tell students to enjoy the refreshments and to spend the next few minutes taking in *God's* messages found in the Bible. Ask volunteers to read the following verses while other volunteers take turns writing down on the projector what God says in each passage. The ideas in parentheses are examples; have students come up with their own.

- Ephesians 2:10 ("You are my masterpiece.")
- John 3:16 ("I love you.")
- 1 John 1:9 ("I desire to forgive you.")
- Matthew 28:20 ("I am here for you.")
- 2 Corinthians 1:18a ("You can trust me.")
- Matthew 10:29-31 ("I notice you.")

Have students continue writing God's messages to them until everyone has been refreshed, both physically (through the snacks) and spiritually (through the truth of God's Word).

continued on next page >>

ministryTOOLS

Get the Message?
(continued)

Now discuss the messages you've explored.

ASK:

- **What thoughts and feelings did you have?**
- **Which of God's messages to you stood out most?**
- **How can you train yourself to better recognize God's messages to you?**
- **How can we "take down" what's not true around us just as we took down the sheet?**
- **How will you respond to these other messages?**
- **How will you respond to God's messages?**

[EXPERIENTIAL WORSHIP IDEA]

Through the Maze

A labyrinth is a path that for Christians represents a spiritual journey; Christians have long used labyrinths for prayer and meditation. Include this kind of spiritual training in your youth ministry.

You might set up Group Publishing's *Prayer Path* or one of Group's Transformation Stations editions to have your students connect with God through a powerful multimedia worship experience (see pages 222-223 for more specifics).

Or you can create your own simple labyrinth as a kind of "praying and reflecting" maze. First find a place where you can use a number of rooms—each one dedicated to a topic or area of life. Topics might include these:

- family situations
- school environment
- friendship
- busyness of life
- expectations (others' and their own)
- things that haunt them (guilt, temptation, and so on)

In each room, set out one lit candle and enough unlit candles for all students. You may also want to have a volunteer or adult leader in each room. Have students move from room to room at their leisure and reflect and pray about each topic.

As each student leaves a room, he or she will light a candle. As students do this, they'll ask God to help them be a light for Jesus and to provide illumination in these areas of their lives so they might see through his eyes.

Have everyone end up in another room or in the main youth area. Read 1 John 1:5-7 together: "This is the message we heard from Jesus and now declare to you: God is light, and there is no darkness in him at all. So we are lying if we say we have fellowship with God but go on living in spiritual darkness; we are not practicing the truth. But if we are living in the light, as God is in the light, then we have fellowship with each other, and the blood of Jesus, his Son, cleanses us from all sin."

Be open to students discussing the experience, but don't force them to share if they'd rather reflect and pray silently. Here are some questions for discussion:

- **What was it like to spend time praying about each of these areas of your life?**
- **What did God teach you through this experience?**
- **How will you commit to spending focused time praying and reflecting?**

You might sing some worship songs or hymns. To end, stand together and thank God for being our light in darkness and our hope as we navigate our lives. Also thank God that he's given you the gift of your group to journey together.

[DEVOTION]

The Sound of Silence

Use this group devotion to help your students put God's Word into practice. This is a vital part of their spiritual training.

Welcome students with lights dimmed and without speaking. Then, still in silence, write Psalm 46:10 on poster board or a dry-erase board.

Tell students that you're all going to experience this verse tonight. Give them a half-hour for complete silence—but don't tell them how long it will be. Expect students to feel awkward and for the mood to be somewhat tense and uncertain. However, maintain the silence and make sure students do as well—if needed, point to the verse you've written. Then use these questions to debrief the experience together:

- **What were you thinking and feeling during this time?**

- **How difficult or easy was this?**

- **What does it mean for you to be still before God?**

- **How can you incorporate meaningful silence into your daily life?**

- **How do you think God will use your silence?**

Commit to including regular and Christ-centered times of silence into your youth group.

(STRATEGY TOOL)

Prayer Blog

Intentionally give students opportunities to spend time with God in prayer. Have a few of your Web-savvy students create a prayer Web log, and share the Web site address with the rest of the group. Make this a place where students can visit often to express to God their most intimate thoughts and feelings.

Emphasize that no commentaries or debates are allowed in the prayer blog; this is purely a place to share prayers, poems, song lyrics, and pictures that are meant for God. Direct students to use this site as a place for frequent prayer and reflection.

Discuss these questions with students:

- **For you, what's the greatest thing about praying? the toughest?**
- **How does God respond to your prayers? How do you feel about that?**
- **How does this prayer blog strengthen your prayer life?**
- **In what other ways can you practice praying more often and more intimately?**

(RESOURCES)

Suggested Resources

Here are some resources to guide your students (and you!) into meaningful spiritual training:

- *Transformation Stations: Giving My Time to God* (Group Publishing)
- *In the Word*, Amy Simpson (Group Publishing)
- *Wearing the Armor of God: 30 119Devotional Experiences* (Group Publishing)
- *Confirming Your Faith: 13 Bible Studies and Rites-of-Passage Experiences for Youth Ministry*, Jim Burns (Group Publishing)
- *Celebration of Discipline*, Richard J. Foster
- *For the Love of God*, D.A. Carson
- *How to Read the Bible for All Its Worth*, Gordon D. Fee and Douglas Stuart
- *The Godbearing Life*, Kenda Creasy Dean and Ron Foster

ministryTOOLS

Chapter 5

COMMUNITY
Building

The Urgency of Friend Making
by Rick Lawrence

Researchers with the National Study of Youth and Religion put a factual face on what most youth leaders are already experiencing: In the competition for teenagers' time, energy, and attention, the church is often losing to school activities, sports, TV, video gaming, and online attractions.

And a lot of community building is happening in each of these secular spheres, making it even more of a challenge to seed deep relational connections in youth groups. According to NSYR lead researcher Christian Smith, very few teenagers form their closest friendships at church.

Now as never before, youth leaders need a determined vision for building community relationships that satisfy teenagers' souls—and point them to Christ.

Leading a Friend-Making Ministry

Ever since Adam and Eve betrayed God and then hid from him, we've been fighting to reclaim intimacy in our relationships. There's no longing that bites harder than our deep desire for friendships that sustain and nurture our soul.

And like us, teenagers live and breathe and move in their relational landscape. They hunger to be known well, understood intimately, and enjoyed for who they really are. If they sense that your ministry knows how to embrace newcomers and has friend building at the core of its DNA, they'll show up. And they'll bring their friends with them.

But friend building isn't safe or easy—another result of living in a fallen world. Real intimacy requires vulnerability and authenticity. Strong communities are made up of students who *bring who they really are* to the youth group. They do that because they sense the four walls of your youth room enclose the safest place in town.

The 1998 film version of Victor Hugo's classic novel *Les Misérables* opens with the ex-convict Jean Valjean trudging toward Dijon, his hometown, after his release from a French hard-labor prison. He's spent 19 back-breaking, soul-crushing years incarcerated for stealing a loaf of bread for his hungry family. Now he has to report to his parole officer in Dijon within four days or he'll be sent back to prison. He stops for the night in an unnamed village—exhausted, alone, and hopeless—and curls up on a hard bench to snatch a few hours of sleep.

An old woman approaches and tells Valjean he can't sleep on the bench. He replies that he's tried the village inn and knocked on every door in town—no one will receive him. She points to a door a few dozen feet away and says, "You haven't tried there—knock on that door." The woman knows that this hardscrabble criminal couldn't have knocked on that particular door because the people behind it would *surely* invite him in.

Desperate, Jean Valjean knocks on the door, which is opened by the town's bishop and his elderly house servant. Valjean asks for food, but the bishop invites him to come inside and share his evening meal. The man branded a criminal pulls out his yellow passport—identifying him as a former prisoner who should be considered dangerous—and tells the bishop he should think twice about inviting him in.

The steely-eyed bishop looks at Valjean and says with gravity, "I know who you are." Shocked, Valjean cautiously enters the bishop's home.

So many teenagers in our culture are just like Jean Valjean—lonely, tired, hurting, and sure they deserve their own "yellow passport," where all their "crimes" and shortcomings are listed in detail. They've stopped longing for true acceptance and true invitation and will gladly settle for some scraps of relational food instead.

So what would it take for your ministry to become known as "the safest place in town," where teenagers who are hungering to be seen and embraced for who they are can learn to let down their guard? As you read this sentence, is something stirring in your soul?

I believe your youth group can and should be the most welcoming place for teenagers in your town. But sadly, the NSYR report and research done by Group Magazine over the years prove that this isn't happening often enough.

Students do not feel like they can be *really* real at church. And that explains why so many Christian teenagers feel comfortable outside of church acting, talking, and thinking in ways that don't reflect a relationship in Jesus, yet they "walk the walk" inside the church.

It's really a pragmatic approach to life. Pragmatism simply means they're behaving in a way that "works" in any given situation.

So what will move students to believe that the church is a good place to talk about the stuff that influences their everyday lives? Wait...not so fast. The question we must explore first is this: Who taught them to hide who they really are at church? Well, we have.

Every Teenager's Secret Desire

Students desperately wish that church could be a welcoming, safe place for them, but most have pretty well decided to guard and protect their "real lives" at church.

That's exactly why Group Magazine decided to discover why teenagers commit, and stay committed, to their church and youth group. We created a questionnaire we nicknamed "The Cool Church Survey" and gave it to more than 10,000 Christian teenagers from across the country.

The survey directed them to rate the importance of 10 factors that influence their commitment to church. We asked, "If you were choosing a church, how important would the following things be?" The factors, and the percentage of teenagers who rated them "very important," included the following:

1. A welcoming atmosphere where you can be yourself—73 percent
2. Quality relationships with teenagers—70 percent
3. A senior pastor who understands and loves teenagers—59 percent
4. Interesting preaching that tackles key questions—53 percent
5. Spiritual growth experiences that actively involve you—51 percent
6. Fun activities—51 percent
7. Engaging music and worship—50 percent
8. Quality relationships with adults—36 percent
9. Multiple opportunities to lead, teach, and serve—35 percent
10. A fast-paced, high-tech, entertaining ministry approach—21 percent

I think the key to understanding these teenagers' responses is at the extremes of the survey—"an atmosphere where I can be myself" at the top end and an "entertaining ministry approach" at the bottom. Students can get all the entertainment they want anywhere, anytime. But they can't get real community anywhere, anytime.

Think for a moment about your youth ministry. Are you spending a lot of time and effort trying to make the time teenagers spend together entertaining, attractive, and flashy? Have you exhausted all your expensive attempts to compete against teenagers' entertainment and media influences—and to capture their attention, their sincere participation, their trust? Well, you can put your mind at rest. When it comes to the kind of Christian community they'll commit to, teenagers aren't hoping for a flashy show, lights and spectacle, or any kind of innovative entertainment.

There's a simpler way to capture their attention, their sincere participation, their trust—and ultimately contribute to their hearts being captured for Jesus. Create an environment that grows and nourishes honest, loving friendship. That's it. Encourage real, raw, transparent relationships in your ministry. If students know they can stop pretending and be who they *actually* are, with people who actually want to know them and love them… well, they're in.

Teenagers Just Want to Be Seen

To understand why teenagers are so desperate to find places where they can be real—where they can experience real community—we have to understand the relational and psychological reality most of them must face every day. Why are so many teenagers so keen to be deeply known and welcomed? The evidence says they experience a world that's full of broken promises, physical and psychological wounding, isolation, confusion, and disconnection.

That's essentially the message of Patricia Hersch's bestselling and heartbreaking book *A Tribe Apart.* Her thesis: Many adults have functionally abandoned their teenagers, in part because of their breakneck, marginless, and self-centered lifestyles and in part because they think teenagers want to be left alone. So in the absence of a warm, nurturing, and purposeful family "tribe," teenagers have formed their own "tribe apart," and this reality has produced lonely, broken, and "unseen" teenagers.

Hersch highlights a compelling truth—for teenagers, nothing is more attractive than "a welcoming atmosphere where you can be yourself." So how do we draw teenagers who have these kinds of needs? It's going to mean pursuing them the way Jesus said his Father has always pursued us.

He made that clear in Luke 15, when he told the parables of the lost sheep, the lost coin, and the prodigal son. Each story highlights the uniqueness, the singleness, and the treasured qualities of the thing sought after. There's a sense in each story that God goes to great lengths to value, see, and rescue individuals. And when he "catches" us, he invites us into intimate relationship with him.

God's relentlessly loving pursuit of our teenagers is the only thing that can build true, intimate, Christ-centered community in our youth groups. And we can be involved in God's passionate pursuit by pursuing teenagers ourselves. Here are two ways to do it.

Passionate Persistence

In the movie *The Horse Whisperer,* Robert Redford plays Tom Booker, a cowboy renowned for his ability to work with difficult horses. He's not a horse psychologist—he just sees them well and, therefore, can reach the painful places that are fueling their damaging behavior. In the film's pivotal scene, Tom is trying to break through with Pilgrim, a horse badly injured after a truck slams into him.

Pilgrim is disfigured and emotionally unstable—the veterinarians advise his owner to destroy the horse but are refused. So Pilgrim lives in the limbo between life and death—too injured, angry, and afraid to be ridden but not so damaged that he can't eat, sleep, and...exist.

Tom attempts to do what others could not—reach past Pilgrim's violent defense mechanisms to calm his fears and heal his wounds. Soon after he begins working with Pilgrim, the horse lashes out at Tom, knocking him down. Pilgrim gallops furiously off into a vast meadow and disappears into a sea of long grass. But Tom picks himself up, walks silently into the meadow, and then hunkers down in the grass to wait on the horse.

Calmly, he kneels and stares at the horse in the distance—not for a few minutes but for the entire day. By dusk, the horse has seen enough. He slowly ambles toward Tom, finally allowing him to stroke his nose and walk him back to the ranch.

This is a story of breakthrough. And it has easy application to powerful youth ministry. Pilgrim is a perfect symbol for many of today's teenagers, who are wounded, afraid, lonely. He dares those around him to see past his abrasive, distancing behavior and touch his soul.

But in a hyperspeed world, who has the time to persist with a hurting student? Often, not the parents or the teachers or the neighbors or the coaches. So a student turns to peers and gets the time he or she is looking for—but not the wisdom or guidance.

The hidden imperative here is that students need someone to commit to them long enough to outlast all their "push away" protective techniques.

How do you answer when a student asks if you have time to talk? If you say yes, it will change the way you schedule your time. It will change your job description. It will change the way you recruit adult leaders. It will change how you reach out to equip parents. It will change your goals for your regular meeting times. It will change how long you stick it out in your current position. It will change what kind of community your youth group is building. It will change everything.

Teenagers are looking for people who are persistent pursuers by their very nature—people who get close to them, learn about them, and become their friends. They're looking for people who act like God.

Passionate Curiosity

Most of us are far more curious about celebrities than we are about the people we live and work with. We're not all that amazed by the personal stories of "average" people, but we'll lean forward to listen to whatever inane thing an actor or singer has to say. This is ridiculous irony since God himself is writing the stories of his people—and there's no better author.

How curious are you about your students' stories? Most teenagers believe it's easy to fool adults because adults rarely are passionately curious about teenagers' lives and therefore have no idea who they are or what their reality is like.

Curiosity is a vulnerable thing, and many of us have been burned so often that we've learned to stop pursuing our curious instincts. We must let that tiger out of his cage again.

Here are a couple of ideas for building community in your youth group through passionate curiosity.

After your weekly meeting, get your volunteers and student leaders together and ask one question: "What did you learn today about the 'real life' of a teenager in our group?"

Do this consistently, like a mantra. Do it so often that your leaders make jokes about it behind your back. Do it so often that it's like breathing for your youth workers to pursue the "real you" in every young person who walks through your door.

Give adult and student leaders a "Challenge Question of the Week" to find out about the students they interact with.

For example: What's something they're angry about this week? What's something that hurt them this week? What's one thing they're proud of this week? You and your team members can brainstorm a list of 52 challenge questions in less than 20 minutes. Then, before each weekly meeting, remind them of that week's question, and encourage them to pursue it with as many students as possible.

With your leadership team, practice asking "the next question."

In conversation, most people don't ask more than one follow-up question. We never "drill deep" in a conversation because we've learned to be lazy. But if you treat each person's everyday story as something God is helping to write, and if you train your leaders to pursue others as if they were Sherlock Holmes trying to solve a mystery (and the mystery is the person in front of them), you'll create a "tipping point" in your ministry's community-building atmosphere.

With your leadership team, practice comfort-producing interactions.

Learn how to notice people so well that you habitually say things to them that prove you see them. This is risky, takes courage, and is powerful. Essentially, you're looking for things that communicate "I enjoy you, and I'm not faking it." It's a two-stage discipline: First, you must train yourself to pay attention to the details and the subtle clues young people reveal about themselves. Second, you must learn to label what you see and name it for that young person. For example, "You know, I loved the way you responded with compassion when Sarah stubbed her toe on the couch today."

Believe in the faith principle behind passionate curiosity and pursuit.

If you believe that your teenagers will open up, they more than likely will. People rise to the level of faith we express in them. When we *expect* our teenagers to do good things that seem risky or potentially embarrassing, they will almost always do it. So coach your leaders to expect teenagers to open up to them in conversation—faith is a choice, not a feeling.

Passionate curiosity will help your students build relationships, think critically, and understand the Bible. How? Passionate curiosity is the foundation for intimacy in relationship—and a truly intimate, Christ-centered community.

Stick to It

Like Pilgrim in *The Horse Whisperer*, many teenagers will initially test your resolve, doubt your intentions, resist your efforts, and resent your pursuit. But in the end, like Pilgrim, most will cave in and open themselves to trust, change, and growth. And, in turn, they will learn to pursue one another in the way that's been modeled for them.

But it's a long process in a world that fights against long anything. So stay with it. Remind yourself of Winston Churchill's great wartime challenge: "When you feel you cannot continue in your position for another minute, and all that is in human power has been done, that is the moment when the enemy is most exhausted, and when one step forward will give you the fruits of the struggle you have borne."

The activities and ideas that follow this page will help you take that next step.

[OBJECT LESSON 1]

The Web of Community

Lead this activity to help students see the power of community. Have groups of eight to 10 students stand up in a circle. Give one person in each circle a ball of string. Have that person hold on to the end of the string, and then toss the ball to another person in the circle. Have each person do the same until everyone in the circle is holding tightly to a section of string.

In the end, there will be a tight web of string between the students.

Allow for some time to reflect on this experience. ASK:

- **In what ways is this like the way people act in a community?**
- **Look at the web between us. How is this like our group? unlike?**
- **What makes a community strong? weak?**

Have one person pull on the string. ASK:

- **What happened?**
- **How is this like our youth group community?**

Have two people let go. ASK:

- **What happens to the web, and how does this affect everyone?**
- **Why do people "let go" of community in real life?**
- **How does this affect others?**
- **What can we do to keep "holding on" in our youth group?**

[OBJECT LESSON 2]

Another Piece in the Puzzle

As a way to kick-start a discussion about Christian community, get an average-size jigsaw puzzle (not too complicated but not too easy). Have each student take a piece of the puzzle and write his or her name on the back. Make sure there are some pieces left over.

Give students time to put the pieces of the puzzle together. Let them struggle through any frustration as they work together.

Afterward, ASK:

- **How did you work together to complete this?**

- **How is this like us working together as a community of Jesus followers?**

Congratulate them for their hard work, and then read together 1 Corinthians 12.27: "All of you together are Christ's body, and each of you is a part of it."

Pray that your group will seek to see the bigger picture and our need for one another. End by praying for the "spaces" in the picture—that God will move into your community and also that you will see God's community of people more clearly.

[APPLICATION IDEA]

Two-Question Conversation

Talk to your group about asking questions and really listening to one another, which are important parts of community building.

SAY: **Anyone can ask a question, and sometimes people ask questions merely to talk about themselves.**

Challenge your students to always ask the other person in a conversation two questions. This will challenge the listener to follow through with a thoughtful second question and will let the one sharing know that he or she is truly being listened to and understood. Give students these two-question examples:

EXAMPLE 1

QUESTION 1:   How was your weekend?

ANSWER: Not too bad.

QUESTION 2:   What was the best part?

EXAMPLE 2

QUESTION 1:   How did your test go?

ANSWER: Not the greatest.

QUESTION 2:   Why do you think that is?

ASK:

- **What's it like when people don't ask questions—and don't listen to what you say?**
- **How do you feel when others ask you questions—and really listen to your answer?**
- **In what ways will practice asking questions and really listening build community in our group?**
- **How will you commit to building a loving community through asking and listening?**

Hide-and-Seek

Try this experience as a way of renewing your students' commitment to community and to each other.

Gather your group at your church, and tell teenagers they're going to play the great childhood game Hide-and-Seek. Ask for a few volunteers to hide, and tell the rest that they'll seek.

Have the hiders hide. While the seekers are counting to 100 in a separate room, pull out a great movie and delicious snacks. Casually ask the seekers to stay and eat; don't directly mention any urgency in finding the hiders. Allow the seekers to think through the options and make their own decisions. See how long it takes the seekers to find the hiders (and if everyone chooses the movie and food, remember to find the hiders yourself!).

Afterward, gather together and process the experience. This was not an activity intended to trick students to "fail," just one that presented two options for students to choose between. So do not make any negative or positive statements about students' decisions. Simply ask questions such as these:

- **Why did you choose what you did?**
- **How did you hiders feel when you were found?**
- **Why do you think people feel like they have to hide sometimes?**
- **When have you felt that way?**
- **How does this "game" resemble a youth group?**
- **Why might people hide and not want to be found?**
- **Why might people look for you?**
- **Why might you hold back and not seek people out?**

SAY: **The purpose of our community here is to stay connected with God and one another. And everyone's help is needed to accomplish that.**

To end, say together: **I need you, and you need me.**

[SMALL-GROUP DISCUSSION]

Here for Each Other

When your teenagers feel like they're part of a real family in your youth ministry, you've accomplished a lot in the area of community building. To help create this "family," intentionally infuse your youth group with the qualities of loyalty, trust, and protection.

First discuss these questions together:

- **What does it mean that we are all brothers and sisters in Christ?**
- **How does that brother and sister relationship come into play when one of us needs help?**
- **How can we be tuned in to others' needs?**
- **In what ways can we actively respond to others' needs?**
- **How can we protect one another? trust one another? be loyal to one another?**

Have students form small groups and brainstorm specific ideas for putting this sense of family into practice. Write all the ideas down. Then post them in your meeting area—and follow through on them as a group.

Students might include these ideas:

- Create a signal for when someone feels uncomfortable or picked on (at school, with strangers, and so on); whoever sees the signal comes to that person's "rescue."
- Have monthly (or more frequent) "family" dinners. Everyone brings something for the meal, and you all spend time talking, laughing, and getting to know one another better.
- Keep a message board where teenagers write prayer requests, concerns, or general updates about how they are.
- Create an "encouragement crew" that puts together cards, gifts, and goodies for students in the youth group who are sick or having a tough time. In a year's time, every teenager should receive one of these care packages at least once.

[SPECIAL EVENT 1]

Mother's Day and Father's Day Remix

Your students' parents play a key role in your youth ministry, so include them in your community-building efforts.

Mother's Day and Father's Day are embedded in our holiday cycle. But sometimes moms and dads "don't feel the love" as their students get older and move toward independence. So take advantage of the holidays to do something special for mothers and fathers. See chapter 6 for more detailed parent ideas, but here is one basic way to build community by honoring parents:

First, explore as a large group what it means to honor parents. Then plan a special time for students to share with their parents what they appreciate about them. Make invitations for the event for students to give to their parents. At the event, have students pray aloud for their parents and give flowers or other gifts to them.

Have those who don't have mothers or fathers in their lives focus on people who love and take care of them (grandparents, mentors, older siblings, aunts or uncles, neighbors, and so on).

Afterward, take some time to discuss these questions with your students:

- **What role do your parents play in our youth group?**

- **Why is it important to include parents in what we do as a community of Christians?**

- **In what ways can you grow closer to your parents?**

- **How will growing closer to your parents affect your relationship with others in the youth group? with God?**

[SPECIAL EVENT 2]

Here-to-There Events

Students often have a tough journey transitioning from grade school to middle school or from middle school to high school. Strategically plan some events that focus on building community for the incoming class. Make it your goal to connect with each student who's participating—and to connect students with one another.

Have older students serve and lead these events, and challenge them to demonstrate their maturity (and coolness!) by hanging out with the younger teenagers.

Examples of here-to-there events include a guys' or girls' night out, weekend camping trip, scavenger hunt, big welcome party, and dedication and commitment service.

After the event, ASK:

- **What memory do you think you'll carry longest from this event?**

- **Why is it important to mark big transitions in life?**

- **How can this kind of experience bring us closer as a group?**

- **What's the next event in your life that you think should be celebrated as a milestone?**

- **What's a transition in life that isn't celebrated but you think should be?**

Celebrating One Another

Make it a habit for your teenagers to celebrate one another—recognizing uniqueness, lifting up successes, and generally being everyone's biggest fans.

Make it a point to discuss the reason for these community-building celebrations. ASK:

- **Why is it important to encourage and celebrate one another?**
- **What effect will celebrating one another have on our youth group community?**
- **In what ways do we please God by being other people's biggest fans?**
- **In what ways does God demonstrate his enthusiasm for us?**
- **Assuming no one in our youth group wins a spot on the All-American team, what makes people worthy of celebration in our group?**

Here are a couple of specific ideas for building community through celebration.

1. Today Is Your Birthday!

Keep careful track of students' birthdays throughout the year. Celebrate each one, and make these celebrations part of your youth group tradition. On each birthday, tell that student, "We're so glad you were born! Life wouldn't be the same without you!"

Here are some ideas for making students' birthdays special:

- Put the birthday person on a chair, and hold him or her up as the group sings "Happy Birthday to You" very loudly.
- Send a card signed by everyone in the youth group.
- Throw a party that features all of the birthday person's favorite food, music, and games.
- Have everyone bring a small and inexpensive gift. Collect all the gifts in a fun container, and present the container to the birthday person as a group.

2. Wall of Fame

Create a "Wall of Fame" in your youth room on which you celebrate every student in the group with photos, funny drawings, appropriate quotes, personal notes, and so on.

Scour the local newspaper daily, and whenever you see the name of any your students, cut it out and put it on the Wall of Fame. The next time you meet, draw attention to the news and celebrate together.

Have everybody contribute to the Wall of Fame so that students form the habit of using encouragement in your community.

[AFFIRMATION IDEA 2]

Nice Guys, Cool Girls

As a way of actively building community, have a "Guys Only" night, at which guys brainstorm some creative ways to encourage the girls in the group. Tell guys that the point is to value them for who God created them to be. Students can use their gifts, interests, or any other resources at their disposal to encourage and affirm the girls. Just make sure to emphasize that this is a secret!

Have the guys follow through on their plan, and the next time around, make it a "Girls Only" night, where the girls creatively encourage the guys.

Afterward, ASK:

- **What's it like to encourage others in this way?**
- **What's it like to be encouraged in this way?**
- **Why does God want us to encourage one another?**
- **How can we build a community of people who affirm and care about one another all the time?**

ministryTOOLS

Question Prompters

To build a caring and God-centered community within your group, you must first understand who your students really are and what they are experiencing.

To find that out, you must ask them questions—often. Give everyone on your ministry team a copy of the "Questions" handout (p. 139), and encourage team members to use it as a tool to begin conversations with students.

You may also want to go over this handout together as a youth group or have students break into small groups to discuss it.

However you use the questions, they're a surefire way to build caring and transparency in your group.

handout on next page >>

Questions

What's one high in your life right now? one low?

Your own question:

What's the best thing that has ever happened to you?

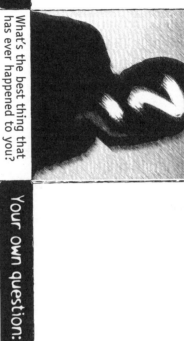

How are you feeling about your family today?

Your own question:

Who's your closest friend in the world? Tell me a story about that friend.

Your own question:

What's the scariest thing that has ever happened to you?

What have you been thinking about the most lately?

Your own question:

How would you describe your relationship with God in three words?

What's your biggest goal in life?

Your own question:

(FIELD TRIP)

Fun and Trust

To develop fun and trust as core values of your youth ministry community, do something together that involves trust, teamwork, and a lot of laughter.

A horseback ride, hike, camping trip, ropes course, blindfolded obstacle course, scavenger hunt, canoeing trip, and white-water rafting trip are all wonderful options.

After the experience, talk together about your students' thoughts and feelings, and talk about how your group can continue to build a strong sense of community. ASK:

- **What were your favorite and least favorite parts of this experience?**

- **How did this experience bring fun and trust to our time together?**

- **How is this like or unlike the kind of trust that's already in our youth group? How is this like or unlike the kind of fun we have together?**

- **What do you fear and enjoy about our relationships in this group, and why?**

- **How can we build more trust and fun into our group?**

- **Which of those things is more important in a community? less important? Why?**

What Is "Big Church"?

Talk with your students about what makes them feel like an important part of your larger church community.

ASK:

- **What gets in the way of you feeling like a part of the church?**
- **What would make you feel like you're important to the church as a whole?**

Listen carefully, and record students' answers.

Alternatively, talk with adults from the church congregation. Ask how they feel about teenagers as part of the church.

ASK:

- **What do you most appreciate about the students? least appreciate?**
- **What role do you think teenagers play in the church as a whole?**

Again, listen carefully, and record the adults' answers.

As a final step, bring both teenagers and adults together to talk about their responses. Discuss the idea of community building across ages and lifestyles, and decide on ways to make everybody a significant and appreciated part of the entire church.

[MINISTRY TEAM IDEA]

Leader Pact

Effective community building often starts with the ministry team. Treat your adult leader and volunteers to dinner, and talk about what it means to be totally engaged—and not engaged—with students at a weekly event, large group meeting, or small group meeting.

Talk about how you can help one another reach out to students, even if it means breaking out of a leaders' "huddle."

Sincerely ask for input, and take every piece of feedback into consideration. Discuss implementing simple suggestions and strategies, such as these:

- Have leaders help out with greeting and with name tags so they make significant contact with students.
- Have leaders form pairs with students for some games and activities. For the newer leaders, this can make things less intimidating.
- Have leaders bring a game or something else they'd love to share with students.
- Encourage them to be involved in all the small-group time and discussions. (Everyone's suspicious of the adult who stands in the back with arms crossed!)

Whatever community-building strategies you decide on, be sure to catch your leaders doing these things well, and thank them.

Also get ideas from students about how your ministry team can help build community in your group. Use these questions:

- **What kind of youth group do you want to be involved in? Describe it in detail.**
- **How can we as youth leaders create a place where you want to be?**
- **What was the time at a youth group function you felt most at home? Be specific.**
- **What was the time at a youth group function you felt most alone and unheard? Be specific.**

[ART IDEA]

In the Zone

Work to make your youth group a community where people lift one another up instead of tearing one another down. In your youth room, put up a sign—or even have students paint a mural—that gets across this idea: "This Is a Negative Free Zone."

Have the students decide together on the best wording and way to reflect this essential aspect of your group's community.

As students work to create this sign, poster, or mural, ASK:

- **What effect does being negative have on someone? What about on the people around that person?**
- **Why isn't it OK to tear someone else down if you're just "being honest"?**
- **What's the true difference between basic negativism and real honesty and transparency?**
- **What does negativism do to a community of Christians?**
- **What kinds of things doesn't God want us to say to one another? Why?**

Ask students to identify specific things that are negative and that could hurt people and the overall sense of togetherness in your group. You might talk about sarcasm, crude jokes, teasing, put-downs, exclusive cliques, lying, and more.

Now explore together what you can do to build intimate and loving community. ASK:

- **What kinds of things does God want us to definitely say to one another?**
- **How does our mural reflect the way people in our youth group treat one another?**
- **How will you contribute to building a positive community in this youth group?**

No matter what you create to express how you'll treat one another as fellow Jesus followers, celebrate that in your group there is safety to be yourself, to be appreciated, and to be loved.

Love and Unity

Lead your students through this interactive community-building experience. Have teenagers form groups of three to five, and ask each group to read 1 John 3 together. Have students focus specifically on what John has to say about the qualities of a community—including love, unity, and so on. Then lead a discussion on the passage. ASK:

- **If John wrote to our youth group today, what do you think he'd tell us we're doing right?**
- **What would he tell us about our unity and love for one another and how it compares with what he observed in Jesus?**

SAY: **Let's put Jesus' command to love one another into action right now. When I say "start," I want you to move around the room and talk to each other. First you'll pair up with someone and tell that person how much you appreciate him or her and why. Be specific! After 30 seconds, I'll tell you to find someone new and start over, so make sure each of you gets a chance to say something within that 30 seconds. Let's take a few minutes to show our love through our words. Start now.**

Every 30 seconds, signal students to pair up with someone new.

When everyone has had a chance to talk to everyone else in the room—or when you run out of time—have students form a circle and join hands. Discuss the experience. ASK:

- **What were you thinking and feeling during this activity?**
- **How does this activity help build the kind of community in our group that John wrote about?**
- **How can we show more unity and love within our youth group?**

End by praying that as your group desires to make an impact on the world around you, you'll love one another first.

Friendship Surrender

Encourage your students to surrender struggling relationships to God and ask him to build love and unity in their relationships.

First have a volunteer read Ephesians 4:2-6 aloud.

ASK:

- **What relationship essentials stood out to you most from this passage?**
- **According to this passage, what are you doing well in your friendships?**
- **How might God want your friendships to be different?**

SAY: **Think silently about a friendship where you're not experiencing some or all of these essentials—love, harmony, forgiveness, peace, unity. It might be a relationship that's been hurt or even broken. Let's take time right now to bring this struggling and broken relationship before God and ask him to heal it.**

Ask everyone to find an object that represents his or her broken or struggling relationship. Students can find objects in the room or take things out of their bags, pockets, wallets, or purses. For example, students might choose a cell phone, set of keys, water bottle, photo, watch, CD, and so on. Provide extra objects for people who don't have anything to choose from.

SAY: **Hold the object in your hand. Offer it to God in prayer, asking him to help you in this specific friendship. Ask God to heal the relationship and take both of you through the struggles and challenges so you can experience the kind of friendship God wants you to have. Ask for peace, harmony, forgiveness, unity, and love. After you've prayed, place the object on the floor as a symbol of surrendering that relationship to God.**

After students have prayed individually and placed their objects on the floor, close in prayer, asking God to help all of you have friendships full of love, harmony, and unity.

[READY-TO-GO FORM]

Create a Youth Notebook

Build a more connected community and help teenagers get to know one another better with a notebook of names and other essential information.

Photocopy the form on page 147. Ask each student to fill out a copy as completely as possible. Then gather all the forms, make copies, and put them in inexpensive plastic three-ring binders. Give each student a copy of the notebook.

Always have blank forms available at your meetings and events so new youth can fill out a form and be included in the notebook. Also be sure to always have copies of the notebook available to hand out to teenagers who are new to your group. Don't forget to photocopy forms turned in by new group members so current members can update their notebooks.

handout on next page >>

[RESOURCES]

Suggested Resources

Here are some resources to build friendships and community in your youth group:

- *Friendship First™: Youth Ministry Kit* (Group Publishing)
- *Friendzee: Close Connections* (Group Publishing)
- *Best-Ever Games for Youth Ministry*, Les Christie (Group Publishing)
- *The 1 Thing*, Thom and Joani Schultz (Group Publishing)
- *Go Team! 101 Ideas to Energize Youth Ministry Volunteers*, Kurt Johnston and Katie Edwards (Group Publishing)
- *Life Together: The Classic Exploration of Faith in Community*, Dietrich Bonhoeffer

Youth Ministry Notebook

NAME:_____

ADDRESS:_____

PHONE NUMBER: _____

E-MAIL ADDRESS: _____

BIRTHDAY:_____

GRADE: _____

MY FAMILY MEMBERS: _____

_____

MY NICKNAMES:_____

MY FAVORITE THINGS TO DO FOR FUN:_____

_____

I'M REALLY GOOD AT:_____

_____

I'D LIKE TO GET INVOLVED IN THE YOUTH GROUP BY: _____

_____

MY FAVORITE FOODS:_____

_____

I STARTED COMING TO THIS YOUTH GROUP IN (MONTH AND YEAR): _____

ONE THING I REALLY WANT A YOUTH GROUP TO HAVE/BE:_____

_____

MY FAVORITE THING ABOUT GOD: _____

_____

WHAT I WOULD LIKE THE REST OF THE YOUTH GROUP TO KNOW ABOUT ME:_____

_____

_____

Chapter 6

...Parents

Partnering With Parents
by Rick Lawrence

The National Study of Youth and Religion affirms and underscores what a growing number of research organizations and youth ministry leaders are emphasizing—that parents are crucial in the faith-development trajectory of their children. When I asked lead researcher Christian Smith about this, he said simply, "You get what you are." The NSYR found that teenagers tend to emulate the religious behaviors of their parents. It's that simple, profound, and...challenging.

Avoiding the Parent Trap

Not long ago, I sat down with a small group of youth leaders from all over the country to talk shop. I asked them what hurdles they were facing in their ministries. Well, the one thing most of them wanted to talk about was how angry and frustrated they were with uninvolved, spiritually apathetic, morally confused, and hyperbusy parents.

It's easy to see why some parents are easy targets—youth leaders have a front-row seat to the pain and destruction brought on by bad parenting. So many parents see the church as a faith "service provider" that will fill their students' faith tank at a bargain price. The worst ones are either incredibly absent from their students' lives or incredibly abusive and harmful.

And it's so easy to respond in the same spirit to those who annoy, vex, and anger us. But we've got to respond to harmful parenting in the "opposite spirit." The opposite spirit means that instead of simply reacting to people in the same spirit they're moving in, you shrewdly upend their momentum and tantalize them into moving in a different direction. Jesus did this all this time.

For example, when the Pharisees brought him a woman caught in the act of adultery (John 8:1-11), they thought they'd devised a perfect way to trap him into saying something contrary to Jewish law. They were looking for a pretext to take him out. Instead, Jesus shocked these smug rule keepers with a response that's the very definition of opposite spirit—"Let the one who has never sinned throw the first stone."

The Primacy of Parents

Youth ministry is desperately in need of people who will move in the opposite spirit toward parents, because parents are the unbeaten kings and queens of impact in their students' lives.

Parents who put forth only a mediocre effort to pass on the great truths of Jesus' gospel to their teenagers still out-impact the greatest youth leader in the world. And that's not an exaggeration.

Some time ago, Group Magazine decided to explore answers to the No. 1 question in youth ministry: "What moves a teenager from a fringe commitment to Christ to a die-for-him commitment?" We pursued this question in a massive survey of Christian students.

The research results confirmed what many other researchers had already discovered—parents matter most in teenagers' growth as Christ followers.

The teenagers in our survey said their parents' impact was by far the biggest "tipping point" in their journey toward a deeper commitment to Christ. We first asked them to mark themselves on a continuum between "fringe commitment" to Christ and "die for him" commitment to Christ. For those teenagers who marked themselves on the second half of the continuum, we asked them to pinpoint the top three reasons their commitment had deepened. Check out the results below.

	Top Reason	2nd Reason	3rd Reason
My parent	17.9%	12.4%	5.8%
A tragedy or crisis or great struggle	14.2%	5.2%	5.0%
My friends	13.9%	9.4%	10.2%
My youth pastor or other adult leader	13.4%	10.7%	6.1%
My participation in a youth group	7.7%	15.4%	10.5%
My experiences at Christian camps or retreats	7.0%	8.1%	11.7%
My participation in service projects or mission trips	5.1%	10.1%	12.0%

Of course, Group Magazine was not the first to shine a bright spotlight on parents' crucial role in teenagers' faith growth. Researchers at the Minneapolis-based Search Institute set out to find the long-term factors that ensured teenagers would stay committed to Christ after high school and into young adulthood. They discovered that two factors were more important than any others: "Talking about faith with your mother" and "Talking about faith with your father."

The point here is this: Parents' spiritual maturity is vitally important when it comes to impacting youth group members for Christ, so it should be every youth pastor's concern, not just the senior pastor's concern. Put another way, it's just as important for you to invest in parents' spiritual growth as it is to invest in your students' spiritual growth.

Aiming Toward Permanent Impact

When we lay down any frustrations we have with parents and create new "opposite spirit" ways to help them teach their students about faith, we've turbocharged our ministry with permanent impact.

The challenge we have to overcome is to convince parents that they're crucial to their students' faith growth—that you must be their partner in ministry, not their faith "service provider." Our job is to find ways to get fathers and mothers engaging with their teenagers about their faith, helping their teenagers wrestle with their doubts, and offering road-sign help on their journey.

Looking for ways to get parents engaged with their teenagers? Here's an idea: Create father-son and mother-daughter experiences that powerfully connect parents and teenagers around their growing faith in Christ.

Denver youth pastors Doug Ashley and Lara Bosler created a six-month program they call "The Wild Challenge," in which fathers and sons navigate key biblical principles with one another. Each month is focused on a different topic and involves experiences and discussion that fathers and sons do together.

You might do something similar in your youth group, fitting the experiences and topics to your teenagers' needs and families.

You might have parents and teenagers...

- go through a Bible study series or set of devotions that you supply. (See the Appendix on page 222 for some great resource ideas!)

- go places together neither of them has ever been before—the farther away the better, since road trips provide awesome conversational opportunities.

- take turns doing or experiencing something that takes them out of their comfort zone (such as a concert, opera performance, cooking lesson, art show, sports event, and on and on!).

- do an activity that requires teamwork, such as rock climbing or navigating a ropes course or blindfolded obstacle course.

- watch a movie together and then discuss it—and relevant spiritual topics—at length (for a wonderful guide to exploring movies through a biblical filter, try *Group's Blockbuster Movie Events*).

- serve others together, which can be anything from volunteering at a homeless shelter or soup kitchen to working in a yard or cleaning someone's house.

- support one another in facing their biggest fears and phobias— going together to a high place and looking down, sitting together in the dark, holding a snake at a petting zoo, and so on.

Encourage parents and teenagers to make prayer an important part of each experience. As they connect with God together, he will strengthen their bond and relationship.

At the end, do what Doug and Lara do: Celebrate with a blessing banquet. This will probably be a tear-filled, emotionally charged time, but it will literally change the trajectories of parent-teenager relationships and mark a new season of life that includes many more natural "conversations about faith" in homes.

Giving Parents What They Deserve

These ideas are prototypical examples of a youth ministry reasserting its God-given role as a parent equipper instead of a parent substitute.

Recently I spoke with Richard Ross, the catalyst for the True Love Waits campaign and a 30-year veteran youth minister. Ross has now sunk his teeth into one of the great challenges in the church today—calling youth pastors to stop their decades-old rivalry with parents and equipping them to reach their own teenagers for Christ.

Together with a small group of local- and national-level youth pastors and influencers, Ross is spearheading a campaign called A Call to Youth Ministers and the Church. It's a battle cry for the church to start partnering with parents instead of competing with them to reach their teenagers. Here's a "gem sampler" of what Ross has to say about moving youth ministries toward a parent-equipping mind-set:

"It is so obvious to those of us that have been doing this awhile that the family environment around young people is a major variable in how things go for them in adulthood…just hanging out with teenagers in a church setting, though valuable, is not enough in terms of shaping their futures…

"I honestly believe the contemporary parent in most congregations now believes his or her primary responsibility in the discipling of a teenager is to faithfully taxi that teenager back and forth to youth group meetings. So not only is there a misunderstanding of a fuller concept of youth ministry on the part of youth leaders, but there is also misunderstanding on the part of parents—and we have to simultaneously call both groups to link arms and learn how to do this differently."

A Time to Train

The shift that Richard Ross talks about sounds daunting, but like any new direction, the point is to build momentum toward your vision. Parents are looking to the church to be an ally in raising their children, not a competitor. So ask your students' parents how your program helps and hurts their family's growth and togetherness. Strengthen what helps; prune what doesn't. And try these ideas:

Help parents reconnect with and re-engage their teenagers.

Our church culture often perpetuates the wider culture's separating impact on students and their parents. In fact, some popular youth ministry models try to build an almost adult-free environment for teenagers on purpose. Ultimately, this hurts teenagers. Take a look at what you're doing that excludes parents, and then brainstorm possible ways parents could be involved.

Go the extra mile to involve parents.

Parents' impact on their teenagers' faith journey will always be stronger than the impact of the best youth ministers in the world. Parents—not the church or the culture or friends—determine their teenagers' long-term faith trajectory.

And that's good news for youth pastors. You can help equip parents to "Direct [their] children onto the right path." Most Christian parents really love their teenagers and want them to grow into committed Christ followers. But they need tools to do the job—they don't lack the desire, though they may lack the knowledge and training.

You can use your God-given gifts for reaching and discipling young people…to help parents reach and disciple their *own* teenagers. See the second part of this chapter for more detailed ideas; here are some brief ones to get your creative gears turning.

- **Keep parents informed.** This means sending them a regular parent newsletter that includes savvy tips on parenting (including faith-nurturing ideas).

- **Keep parents connected.** This means creating a "Parent Support Network" in your church where parents can get practical training for engaging their teenagers in faith-growing conversations.

- **Keep parents affirmed.** This means praising and showcasing great examples of parenting in your church.

- **Keep parents resourced.** This means connecting parents with great books, videos, and audio tapes that will help them in their difficult calling (see these kinds of tools on page 173).

- **Keep parents spiritually supported.** This means fighting for your students' parents in prayer.

- **Keep parents easily involved in the ministry.** This means making it free for at least some of them to join you on mission trips and retreats.

Treat parents as your primary ministry focus.

What do you think the parents of your students most need to hear? Here's another way to get at that question—right now, take five minutes to write a list of your top complaints about the parents in your church. Then, next to each complaint, write the challenge that must be overcome if you hope to partner with parents in your ministry. For example, let's say you wrote that parents see your ministry as a baby-sitting service. The challenge you'd have to overcome is convincing parents that they're crucial to their teenagers' faith growth—that you must be their co-partner in ministry, not their ministry provider.

After you've listed the challenges, start brainstorming ways to overcome each one. This will then become a loose framework for structuring your ministry to primarily target parents.

Shifting Your Paradigm

Don't believe the myth that your job is to work yourself out of a job. The truth is that the more you commit to equipping parents, the more support and training you'll need to give them. You'll simply cut back on hands-on skills with students and increase your investment in parents. Your job will become more, not less, invigorating and satisfying as you make the shift.

And the ideas that follow this page will help you make the transition.

Family Dinner

Host a meal at which students serve the parents by hanging up coats, pulling out chairs, and serving the drinks and meal. Depending on the number of people present, have students come up front at some point during the event and share a pre-written statement of appreciation for their parents.

Provide a "Family Dinner" handout (p. 157) to each family member so answers can be shared at the table during the meal. These open-ended and lighthearted questions will strengthen the relationship between parents and teenagers.

BONUS IDEAS

Ahead of time, videotape various people—adults and students—doing 30- to 60-second "spots" affirming your students' parents. Show these sometime during the dinner.

You may also tape students thanking their parents for seeing them through a hard time, encouraging them in their walks with God, setting a good example at home, or just loving them unconditionally.

Finally, you may videotape yourself and other youth leaders thanking the parents of your teenagers. On camera, thank parents for letting their teenagers be part of your youth ministry. Share funny and touching stories about their children. Tell them what you see in their children and thank them for doing the overwhelming, sometimes exhausting, job of raising their teenagers.

Then either show the footage or present parents with copies of the tape as gifts.

handout on next page >>

1 How would your family say you **wake up in the morning?**

2 Are you a **picky eater?** What food would your family say is your least favorite?

3 Which family member is most likely to **take forever in the bathroom?**

4 Who is the **funniest person** in the family? Share an example of what that person says or does that's so funny.

5 What's one of your **favorite things** about your parent/son/daughter?

6 What's your favorite thing about **your family?**

7 What do you see when you imagine your family in **10 years?**

8 What **special gift or skill** does your parent/son/daughter have?

9 If you could let your parent/son/daughter **know one thing** about you, what would it be?

10 What five words would other family members use to describe you?

[NEWSLETTER IDEA]

Dear Parents

Group Magazine provides online parent newsletters that can be copied and mailed to parents. If you make one of your own, include specific info for your youth ministry and church. Also include a schedule for the coming month (or quarter); any costs for events; and a short list of volunteers and adult leaders, along with the ages they work with and small groups they lead.

Finally, include a brief personal paragraph from you or another youth leader. This can highlight a specific Bible verse or theme students are studying. It can also offer a parenting skill and a note of affirmation, appreciation, or encouragement.

[READY-TO-GO FORM]

Behind-the-Scenes Parents

Have parents who would like to be involved in a less-visible capacity set up a rotating "Behind-the-Scenes Support" program. Promote this idea during announcements in the worship service or with bulletin inserts. Provide a checklist of capacities in which a parent can be involved (sample on page 159).

Openly communicate your genuine desire for parents' involvement—and gratitude for whatever they do. Make sure parents know that "Not only do we need you as part of this ministry, but we also *want* you to be a part of this ministry!"

handout on next page >>

Behind•the•Scenes Support

How do YOU want to be involved in the youth ministry?

☐ Setting up for weekly meetings

☐ Chaperoning events or retreats

☐ Praying behind the scenes

☐ Picking up needed supplies and materials

☐ Making phone calls and sending e-mails

☐ ....
....
....

☐ Any of the above

Parent Seminar

Host a parenting seminar as inexpensively as possible, especially targeting single parents and students' parents who don't regularly attend your church. Provide a pleasant, warm atmosphere with refreshments. Have students or adult volunteers greet parents and show them to their seats.

Begin by telling them that you and your youth ministry team care about them and their families.

Invite an outside speaker (or use two or three parents in your congregation) to give talks on preselected topics relevant to attendees. Include a panel of parents in one session for open questions. Here are suggestions for topics:

- single parenting
- discipling your own child
- boundaries with teenagers
- choosing the right college
- maintaining a healthy marriage for the sake of a healthy teenager
- understanding your teenagers' faith
- how to engage your teenagers about their culture
- insights into how your teenager's brain really works
- creative rites of passage
- parenting with love and logic

Notecard Party

Make encouraging parents a big part of your ministry.

It's easy to catch them just before or after church and say something like, "Hey, Alex was cracking us up as usual in small group last week. I just want to tell you how much we enjoy having him. I'm glad you let him be involved; it wouldn't be the same without him."

You can take it a step further by writing similar sentiments in a notecard now and then. Plan a "notecard party" with your adult leaders.

Purchase small, inexpensive notecards with envelopes, or have someone who does scrapbooking make postcards on card stock purchased from a hobby store. Meet somewhere with a big table or large floor area. Begin by praying and thanking God for each parent.

Next, evenly distribute the notecards among you. On each card, one of you can write a brief, specific, and uplifting note to a parent. Here are things to let parents know:

- You're aware that they have the greatest responsibility in their children's lives.
- You respect them. A lot.
- You and your team pray often for them.
- You're rooting for them!

You may also want to list some Scripture passages on the notecards. Here are a few suggestions:

- Deuteronomy 6:5-7
- Deuteronomy 11:18-19
- Proverbs 17:6b
- Proverbs 20:7

[AFFIRMATION IDEA 2]

Encourage Them

At your next parent meeting or student-parent event, show a clip from *Cheaper by the Dozen*. These two scene ideas illustrate the value of family and affirm the parents' investment in their teenagers' lives. Here are a couple of suggestions for the clips and doing post-watching affirmations.

Reword the suggestions to fit your style and your group of parents. After each affirmation, have youth leaders and students gather around the parents and pray for them.

MOVIE ILLUSTRATION 1:

Cue the movie to 1:12:40. The father (Steve Martin) is reading a letter from the school informing him that his eldest son, Charlie, has been kicked off the football team. Charlie is unhappy about moving to a new town he doesn't fit into, and he blames his father. The father barges into Charlie's room, and they argue about Charlie wanting to quit school. Charlie says some hurtful things to his father, finally telling him, "When I graduate, I'm gone." Stop the scene at 1:14:10 when Dad throws the school letter down.

AFFIRMATION: "As parents, you have to make tough decisions on behalf of your families. Unfortunately, you can't always predict how those decisions will affect each family member. Sometimes your teenagers blame you for their unhappiness and say hurtful things. It stinks when you act like a parent and you're treated like the enemy. But deep down inside, your students probably know that you make decisions based on what's best for them.

"We showed this clip because we wanted to remind you that we recognize the incredible responsibility you have in your teenagers' lives. We don't assume that it's easy. Parenting costs far more than money. Yet by the way we see some of you interacting with your teenagers, it's obvious that the cost is worth it to you. You're not perfect, and your children probably have methods of illuminating that to you. But in ways that others don't see, you sacrifice for them. And we just wanted to acknowledge you for that and tell you how much we admire and support you."

MOVIE ILLUSTRATION 2:

Cue the movie to 1:19:30, when one of the younger Baker children is sad about his dead frog. No one in his family seems to care because everyone's preoccupied.

The oldest sister, Nora, thinks Mark may have taken a train to go back to Midland, "his favorite place in the world." We see the father running through the train station, finding him on the train, and tearfully embracing him. This is a powerful scene about a father's love and could stand alone if you're talking specifically to fathers. Stop at 1:24:10 before the scene changes from the train to the train station.

OPTIONS: Continue to the following scenes of the father watching the children snuggling with Mom and then resigning the next day in Shenk's office, saying, "If I screw up raising my kids, nothing I achieve will matter much." Either end before the scene changes or continue to the next-to-last scene with the narrator's voice-over about the number 12: "And each day, it's the number of times I'm thankful there's such a thing as family."

AFFIRMATION: "Maybe your family has experienced personal crises. Maybe a few of those crises didn't have the warm-fuzzy ending that scene did. We showed this clip simply to say that we recognize that God has given you the job of raising your children. We youth workers don't presume we could do your job better or have greater influence over your students than you do. We just want to affirm you, the parents. And we want to say *thank you* for doing your best when you don't necessarily see the results you'd like or get the appreciation you deserve. Thank you for letting your great teenagers be part of this youth ministry. We joke a lot around here, but we mean it when we say that your teenagers are a delight to us. We love them, and we just want to say to you, the parents, 'Ya done good.' "

Parent Get-Together

Some youth leaders host a parent meeting when they first start at the church to allow parents to get to know them. Others hold an annual parent meeting as part of their ongoing ministry. But we're suggesting you not go this route. Because an annual meeting is a bad idea? No...not unless your plan is to ask parents to voice their concerns and ideas, wait them out while they talk, and then proceed to tell them where you're coming from and what you plan to do in youth ministry—and expect them to fully support you.

Your regular parent meeting, whether it is annual, biannual, or quarterly, is just a starting point to build relationships throughout the rest of the year. Having your senior pastor present is a key element to your meeting. Here are other things to include beyond "next year's schedule of events":

- Have a specific time of prayer for and with the parents, being aware that not all may be Christians.

- Read aloud Scripture that affirms them in their essential role as parents.

- Talk about your priorities and goals for leading the youth group.

- Keep time on the agenda for questions from parents.

- Be specific in your words of affirmation. You may even say something like this: "Most of you already know this, but you might need a reminder that we in youth ministry recognize you, the parents, as the No. 1 influence in your children's lives. It's not us, their friends, their teachers, or anyone else—it's you. Don't hold your breath waiting for your teenagers to admit this, but we want you to know that we know it! And we want to tell you that we're honored that you trust us to make a small investment in their lives."

[MINISTRY STRATEGY 2]

Tuesdays With Morrie...
Er...You

Block out a one- or two-hour time slot to meet with parents every month—or each week, if you're able. Alternate between a morning and afternoon time to accommodate parents' schedules. Call it "Tuesdays With Morrie...Er...YOU" or some other creative and inviting name.

Send an e-mail or postcard letting your students' parents know you'd love to meet with them, hear their concerns, pray for them, get their feedback, and simply get to know them better.

Choose a coffee shop or fast-food place in a neutral location, and let parents know you'll be there during a certain time frame. Call specific parents you'd like to meet with in particular. Be ready with a list of suggested parent helps (books and resources) in the form of a bookmark. If you give it to everyone, no one will think you're insinuating they aren't "doing their job" as parents.

Also let this be your opportunity to ask these parents about their strengths and gifts—to see if they might be willing to be a behind-the-scenes prayer partner for the youth ministry, a now-and-then chaperone for a retreat, or a volunteer youth sponsor for a season.

If you're concerned that a certain parent may come to you with more gripes than you can handle in one shot, bring your spouse or a trusted adult leader or staff member for moral support.

Quotes to Parent By

Read through these quotes, and then spend a few minutes praying that God will bless each student's parents and build the parent-teenager relationship. You might also consider sharing these quotes with parents to spark meaningful discussion.

"As Christian parents, we can't afford to define normal by what the rest of the world considers common behavior. If we do, our teens can get pretty confused too."

—Stephen Arterburn and Fred Stoeker with Mike Yorkey,
Preparing Your Son for Every Man's Battle

"The idea that rebellion is necessary in order for a child to become an adult offers a false sense of comfort to bewildered parents, freeing them from accountability for their teen's behavior...Adolescence *is* a time of self-discovery. But discovery doesn't have to mean defiance."

—Gary Ezzo and Dr. Robert Bucknam,
On Becoming Teenwise

"Your task as a parent is to help your child develop inside him what you have been providing on the outside: responsibility, self-control, and freedom."

—Dr. Henry Cloud and Dr. John Townsend,
Boundaries with Kids

"Don't fall prey to the rumors that teenagers are trouble or are hard to live with. Everybody is trouble and hard to live with, at least from time to time."

—Karen Dockrey,
Reaching Your Kids

"Despite the fact that parents and teenagers seem to communicate on very different levels, it is a must that both teenagers and parents work on making the communication thing happen...as you well know, there are moments, glimpses if you will, when you see that quality communication is possible. It just takes a lot of work."

—Jim Burns,
Parenting Teenagers for Positive Results

[WRITING IDEA]

To My Parent

Use this idea to help students honor their parents and honestly express their thoughts and feelings.

Have students find a quiet, private spot in the room. Give each student a "To My Parent" handout (p. 168) and a pen. (Feel free to create another letter starter with different questions.)

Ask everyone to write a letter to a parent (or to both parents). Tell students they won't give the letters to their parents unless they want to, so they can be completely honest and write from their hearts. Be available during this time to help teenagers word their letters, if asked.

Have students present letters to their parents at a family night or parent-child event. Another idea is to have students mail the letters to their parents' places of work or slip the letters under their parents' pillows, in their briefcases, or another surprise place.

Discuss these questions:

- **How easy or difficult was it to write this letter? Why?**
- **What did you learn about your parents—or your relationship with your parents—through this experience?**
- **In what ways will this letter make your relationship with your parents better?**
- **How can you better love and encourage your parents?**

BONUS IDEA

You might provide ribbon so students can roll up their letters like scrolls and tie them. Or provide craft supplies for students to decorate the envelopes in which they'll put the letters.

handout on next page >>

ministryTOOLS

To My Parent

Dear ....

I want to thank you for..

....

....

I want to ask you to forgive me for ....

....

....

I need to forgive you for ....

....

....

What I love most about our relationship is..

....

....

The thing I want most to improve in our relationship is ....

....

....

You can help me in my relationship with God by..

....

....

Heart-to-Heart

This is the face-to-face version of the "To My Parent" letter. Do this at a father-son, mother-daughter, or parent-student retreat. Your goal is to make it easy for parents and students to be open and humble with one another.

First, read aloud Colossians 3:13: "Make allowance for each other's faults, and forgive anyone who offends you. Remember, the Lord forgave you, so you must forgive others."

Then have each family head to a private section of the room. Encourage eye contact as much as is comfortable. Let participants know that you'll begin this interaction by starting the sentences you wish them to complete and giving a certain amount of time to complete the sentences.

If there's more than one sibling in a family, leave it to the family's discretion as to how they share this interaction. Some will want to do this altogether, some individually.

For the "forgiveness" portion of this experience, instruct them to listen to each other without interrupting. Tell them that they may not explain or justify any actions until the activity is over. At that time, it's acceptable to ask the person to let them explain themselves.

Be clear that the idea is reconciliation and understanding—not excuse-making and defending. Sometimes it doesn't matter why something offends; it matters that there is mutual respect between people. This could be a powerful exercise in healthy families. In dysfunctional families, it could be like ripping scabs off old wounds. You know your group best, so be wise, prayerful, and discreet in your directions.

Have parents go first and then students.

- Ask parents to finish the sentence "I want to thank you for..." Students should simply respond, "You're welcome" and then say to their parents, "I want to thank you for..." as well.
- Next, have parents finish the statement "I want to ask you to forgive me for..." If they're not sure, they can ask, "Is there anything I've done to hurt you that I need to ask forgiveness for?" and then be quiet and listen. Instruct students to respond, "I forgive you." (Let them know ahead of time that if there are serious issues too difficult to work through in this exercise, you will be available either to talk with them privately and mediate or to connect them with a mature couple who will help them work through it.) Next, lead students in the same exercise, focusing on asking their parents' forgiveness.

continued on next page >>

Heart-to-Heart (continued)

Sensitively watch to make sure most of the families are finished before moving on.

• Then instruct parents to say, "The thing I want most to improve in our relationship is…" and finish that sentence. When the parents are finished sharing, students can respond, "Thank you. I'll work on…" and finish the sentence. Finally, reverse the roles with students saying the same thing to parents.

Play instrumental worship quietly in the background. Close by having parents pray for their children and students pray for their parents.

(TOPIC EXPLORATION)

Dating My Parents' Way

To involve parents in their teenagers' exploration of relationships and dating, have several parents join you when you discuss these important topics as a group. Invite parents who will represent all kinds of different experiences and dating stories. Be sure to include parents who are single, divorced, and married.

Ask parents to share funny anecdotes, embarrassing moments, and thought-provoking memories. Have them get up one at a time (individually or as a couple) to share their stories.

Take this idea a step further by having students ask the parents questions about dating, relationships, sex, and marriage itself. Slot 15 to 20 minutes at the end of the time to have a Q-and-A session with the parents. Be prepared for personal questions and very truthful answers.

Here's an idea you can use before your "Dating My Parents' Way" panel or as a stand-alone idea before you speak on purity or dating.

Provide the following handout of questions (p. 171), and have your students "interview" one or both of their parents individually. Use your discretion in having students share with the group some of their parents' funnier or more insightful answers (those that don't violate parents' privacy). Note that some of these questions are obviously geared toward two-parent homes, and some are obviously geared toward single parents. An option would be to provide a separate set of questions for single parents (removing the obvious questions geared toward two-parent homes).

handout on next page >>

ministryTOOLS

Dating My Parents' Way

1. When and where did you and Dad/Mom meet?

2. What attracted you to Dad/Mom?

3. What irritated you about Dad/Mom when you were dating?

4. What was the defining moment when you knew you wanted to marry him/her?

5. How have you seen him/her grow in your marriage?

6. How have you grown since marrying Dad/Mom?

7. How does your relationship with God affect your marriage to Dad/Mom?

8. *(Optional)* How have you grown since the divorce? (If a student is young or the divorce is recent, we encourage skipping this question.)

9. *(Optional)* How have you grown since Dad/Mom died? (If a student is young or the death is recent, we encourage skipping this question.)

10. What is the most important piece of advice you think every teenager should know about dating?

11. What is one of the most important pieces of advice you think every teenager should know about marriage?

Date Nite

Use this idea to encourage one-on-one time between parents and students.

If students have younger siblings, find volunteers who will baby-sit for free so the parents and teenagers can go out on a "date."

Once you've set up any necessary child care, call or write parents to let them know you're encouraging them to do this get-together because you value their relationships with their teenagers. If they're looking for ideas of what to do, provide a short list of suggestions: bowling, a meal, coffee and dessert, window-shopping at the mall, a bike ride, a museum trip, a hike, and so on. (Discourage going to a movie since this activity isn't conducive to interaction.)

You might provide a short list of questions for parents and students to go over during their time together. Here are some possible questions:

- **When was your first kiss and with who?**

- **What was your most embarrassing moment as a child?**

- **What was your most recent embarrassing moment?**

- **If you could change anything about yourself, what would it be?**

- **If your dream job paid a million dollars a year, what would you do for a living?**

- **What have you always wanted to do but thought it was too crazy or expensive?**

- **How can I love you better?**

- **How can I pray for you?**

- **What's your greatest wish for your relationship with Jesus?**

Follow up with your students after the get-togethers. Ask what it was like for them, and urge them to continue to spend one-on-one time with their parents.

Suggested Resources

Having great resources on hand will strengthen your co-ministry with parents *and* serve the parents of your students. Keep a few full shelves of books and media resources that parents can use to help them in their parenting adventure.

You might even type up a list of recommended books, media products, and Web sites on a homemade bookmark (just a half-sheet of colored paper) that parents can take with them when they borrow items. Your investment in parents will speak volumes (pun intended)!

Here are a few suggestions to start building your parent shelf:

• *Plugging In Parents* (Group Publishing)

• *Parenting Teenagers for Positive Results*, Jim Burns (Group Publishing)

• *Boundaries with Kids*, Dr. Henry Cloud and Dr. John Townsend

• *On Becoming Teenwise*, Gary Ezzo and Dr. Robert Bucknam

Suggested Web Sites

• www.youthministry.com

• www.ministryandmedia.com (exploration of media and culture)

• www.cpyu.org (Center for Parent/Youth Understanding)

• www.parentministry.org (Parenting Teenagers)

• www.wildfrontier.org/mompop.htm (Wild Frontier)

• www.homeword.com (HomeWord)

• www.christianitytoday.com/parenting (Christian Parenting Today)

• www.christiansingleparents.com/resources.htm (Christian Single Parents)

Chapter 7

OUTREACH AND Evangelism

Reclaiming Evangelism
by Rick Lawrence

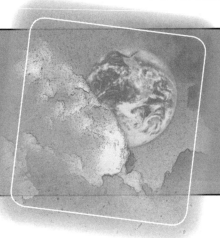

According to the results of the National Study of Youth and Religion,

more than half (54 percent) of all American teenagers think it's OK for people to evangelize others into their faith.

So though they live in a culture that's militantly "diverse," teenagers are not as closed as we think to "classic" evangelism. That means an even higher percentage of them would be open to, at the very least, a respectful conversation about differing beliefs. In John 4:35, Jesus urged his followers to recognize "harvest time": "You know the saying, 'Four months between planting and harvest.' But I say, wake up and look around. The fields are already ripe for harvest."

Essentially, he's telling them that many people are like fruit waiting to be plucked, so get busy plucking! And the results from the NSYR show we're living in a time when our fields are just as ripe for harvest as ever.

The Straw Man of Evangelism

A straw man is literally a dummy in the shape of a man created by stuffing straw into clothes. Straw men have been used as scarecrows, combat-training targets, and effigies for burning. But metaphorically a straw man is a fake target used by an opponent to "win" an argument.

Let's say, for example, that conventional wisdom says the biggest hindrance to evangelism and outreach today is the wholesale antagonism teenagers have toward people who try to "convert" them. If you accept this straw man as the real problem, you'll quickly argue that our culture's obsessive fixation on "diversity" is the real culprit. And you'll waste your time trying to fight a close imitation of the true challenge.

Results of the NSYR show teenagers are mostly open to listening to the claims of Christ—they're not nearly as put off by the gospel's "exclusivity" as we assume. So the "evangelism antagonism" theory for why teenagers stay on the evangelism sideline is really a straw man.

Walking the Talk of Evangelism

In the United States, youth ministers almost always say "equipping my students to share their faith with their friends" is among their top five goals. But in my work as Group Magazine's editor, I've learned that almost half of them don't practice what they prioritize. Faith sharing and outreach training are always near the bottom of their list of "common elements in my youth ministry programming."

So are most youth leaders liars? Of course not—just the opposite is true. You're likely braver, smarter, more energetic, and more committed to the truth than your non-youth leader friends. And here's the evidence: You watch TV shows you'd rather not, play games you're too old to play, stay up way later than your personal curfew, and endure unfounded criticisms just so you can win the chance to introduce Jesus to teenagers.

So what's going on here? To help rediscover true outreach in our ministries (the way God wants us to do it), let's kick around some possible reasons.

We may not be all that certain anymore of who Jesus is and what he came to do.

Have you ever really stepped back from the nuts and bolts of youth ministry and assessed the big picture? It's great to equip youth leaders with ideas and strategies that will draw more teenagers to Jesus, but who is the Jesus you're actually introducing to students?

Many of us are calling students to Hamburger Helper Jesus—we essentially tell teenagers that Jesus is this mix of good stuff (the real meat) they can simply add into their lives to make them better. First-century Christians would scoff at this notion—Jesus asked his followers to die for him. He wanted it all.

Look at the disturbing story of Ananias and Sapphira (Acts 5:1-15). Because they pretended to give everything, they paid with their lives. The result? "Great fear gripped the entire church," and "no one else dared to join [the believers]." Well, of course. A lot of people who wanted to fit Jesus into their lives were repelled when they learned that the price for following him was…everything.

The solution: We'd better make sure the Jesus we're calling students to is really Jesus. For example, several years ago Group Magazine asked thousands of Christian teenagers to answer some questions about basic Christian beliefs. By happy mistake, the survey was also given to a few hundred Christian adults, too. The results from the teenagers were disappointing, but the results from the adults were downright shocking. Of these adults,

- more than a quarter (28 percent) said the Bible is not totally accurate in all it teaches and that Satan is just a symbol of evil, not a living spiritual being.
- one in five (19 percent) said a person can earn salvation through good deeds.
- one in eight (13 percent) said that Jesus committed sins while he lived on earth.

Now these are certainly not the only "measurables" for an authentic faith in Christ. But the take-away here is obvious—to the extent we are confused and just plain wrong about Jesus and his gospel, our students will be, too.

We used to have "faith-sharing templates" that made sense and worked, but not anymore.

To people doing youth ministry a long time, it may seem like the gospel story used to be so easy to understand and so simple to communicate. But today's culture wouldn't agree with the bumper sticker popular with Christians many years ago—"One Way." Faith in Jesus Christ is a viable option in our culture but certainly not the only one. And traditional, simplistic faith-sharing tools seem ineffective. We sense that those tools don't work anymore, but we have nothing to replace them.

The solution: Somehow, we need to re-embrace the essentials as we equip our students to reach their peers for Christ. Jesus is the *only way* to salvation, and he asks his followers to give up *everything*. That's exactly why "the gateway to life is very narrow and the road is difficult, and only a few ever find it" (Matthew 7:14).

Some in the church may have forgotten the purpose of the church.

There seems to be a disturbing shift of focus in the United States from biblical goals and culture to congregational goals and culture. Some churches have made it very clear they don't really want unchurched teenagers co-mingling with their teenagers. Some ban skateboarders from their parking lots. Some insist that teenagers keep all or most of their own culture out of the church. Some worry about unchurched teenagers' impact on churchgoing students instead of relishing the opportunity for Jesus-following students to deeply impact their unchurched peers.

The solution: Christ-like subversion might mean asking at staff meetings and church board gatherings, "What is our church's determined vision for reaching those who don't have a relationship with Christ? Which of our cultural boundaries are we willing to relax in order to reach unchurched teenagers?"

We've valued disciple making but haven't always practiced it.

We haven't lost our passion for evangelism, but we have lost much of our vision for teaching it. And our students are losing their ability to pass on core truths because they're rarely in a position to tell others about them.

Youth ministry educators Dave Rahn and Terry Linhart, co-authors of the book *Contagious Faith*, did extensive on-site research among youth groups that evangelize well. They were trying to learn why some groups are successful at leading teenagers to follow Jesus and others are not.

The solutions:

- **We must start with role modeling.** In short, we have to show them how to share what it means to have a relationship with Jesus. "As leaders," Rahn and Linhart write, "if our walk with Christ doesn't include a focus on prayer and evidence of our desire to share our faith with our peers, there's a good chance students won't develop a desire to pray and share their faith with friends...youth leaders set the pace for their youth ministries."

- **We must give teenagers opportunities to practice prayer.** Young people must have regular practice praying. You can do this by making corporate and individual prayer a dominant part of your regular meetings, by creating prayer reminder cards and laminating them so students can carry them around, or by introducing your group to the "24-7 Prayer" Web site (www.24-7prayer.com) and getting them involved in a crazy, impractical, life-changing prayer movement.

- **We must "invite well" by creating an atmosphere that expects young people to bring their non-Christian friends.** It's no surprise—youth ministries that do well at leading people to relationships with Jesus spend a great deal of time training teenagers to welcome and reach out to their peers.

- **We must commit to verbally telling others about Jesus.** Groups that do well at sharing the gospel practice it often. Weekly training times that include practical experience in telling others about God's grace and forgiveness (not just modeling it) are the common thread. Many of us have taken comfort in this famous quote from St. Francis of Assisi: "Preach the Gospel at all times and when necessary use words." But we also need to understand the right balance: In an era of blurred spiritual distinctions, words *are* necessary.

• **We must be sensitive to the poor and hurting—those Jesus targeted in his "outreach" efforts.** Jesus spent almost all his time and ministry energy on desperate people. And Jesus-style youth groups are similarly passionate about welcoming strangers and outcasts—when they do, they teach teenagers the heart of Jesus. About 90 percent of this is accomplished through modeling. If your leaders (adults and students) are fanatics about welcoming, enjoying, and pursuing everyone who walks through your door, the whole group will slowly adopt what it sees as a core value.

According to the Communities In Schools organization, three out of five teenagers (60 percent) who get meaningful attention from adults say they're "very happy," compared with just over a third (37 percent) of those who say they get much less attention from adults. And two-thirds of adult-pursued teenagers (66 percent) rate themselves as "extremely healthy," while only 5 percent of those who get less adult attention feel the same way.

Truths About Faith Sharing

A few years ago, respected Christian pollster and cultural commentator George Barna stirred the youth ministry pot by trying to make a case for a massive shift of church resources out of youth and adult ministry and into children's ministry. New research, he said, proves that just 4 percent of all Christians committed their lives to Christ when they were teenagers.

"The statistics are eye-opening," wrote Barna, "because they show how little evangelistic impact we are having in America upon teenagers and adults." In addition, the survey report charged, "The data also challenge the widely held belief that the teenage years are prime years for evangelistic activity."

Soon after Barna's report was released, Group Magazine partnered with Dave Rahn and the Youth Ministry Educators organization to come up with a small-scale research project to learn more about the role of youth ministry in students' relationships with Jesus. We designed a seven-question survey that youth ministry professors gave to 369 Christian students on 10 campuses across North America.

Here are the results of that study:

1. How old were you when you first decided to put your trust in Jesus Christ as your Lord and Savior?

13 or younger: 63 percent

Between 14 and 18: 29 percent

19 or older: 8 percent

2. When you think about how you came to faith in Christ, did it happen in an instant as it did with St. Paul, or did it happen over a longer period of time as it did with St. Peter?

St. Paul: 23 percent

St. Peter: 77 percent

3. Do you remember a subsequent moment in time—perhaps almost as personally significant to you as your conversion—when your commitment to Christ was especially launched or solidified?

13 or younger: 10 percent

Between 14 and 18: 59 percent

19 or older: 20 percent

Doesn't apply to me: 11 percent

4. Describe that significant experience.

Most frequent responses, in order...

1. mission/service trip

2. crisis experience

3. big event

4. camp experience

5. going away to college

6. teaching others about Christ

7. the example set by other Christians

8. a Holy Spirit experience

5. Who or what has been most instrumental in influencing your present commitment to Christ?

Most frequent responses, in order…

1. youth leader

2. parents

3. friends

4. other adult (employer, teacher, relative)

5. brother or sister

6. church pastor

6. Can you identify a point in time when honest reflection caused you to really question whether you were truly committed to Christ?

13 or younger: 5 percent

Between 14 and 18: 42 percent

19 or older: 31 percent

Doesn't apply to me: 22 percent

7. Describe who or what helped you through this transitional stage of your faith in Jesus Christ.

Most frequent responses, in order…

1. friends

2. family

3. youth pastor

4. Bible or other book

5. professor

In short, many people may vividly remember the first step they took toward an intimate relationship with Jesus. But must that one moment define and confine their Christian-growth trajectory? No way! As with the several hundred Christian college students who responded to this faith journey survey, that experience constitutes just a tiny chapter in a person's faith story.

So here's what we can pull out and apply to outreach and faith sharing in our own youth ministries.

Family ministry is the key to sharing faith in Jesus.

The percentage of Christians who say they first committed their lives to Christ when they were children is slightly lower than Barna's survey number—but the breakdown generally matches his findings. Most people in America make faith commitments to Jesus because their parents bring them to church regularly when they're young. Parents are, by far, the best faith sharers, evangelizers, and outreachers (if there even is such a thing).

Teenagers need recommitment experiences like rockets need boosters, and you are key to those experiences.

Three-quarters of our respondents said they made a faith commitment to Christ over a long period of time, belying the "one moment in time" stereotype that dominates our thinking. Nine out of 10 said they, indeed, had a crucial recommitment experience that was as significant as their initial step toward Jesus. And two-thirds of these folks said their experience happened when they were teenagers.

Mission trips where teenagers do something in the name of Jesus, crisis experiences where teenagers learn that they deeply need Jesus, big events where teenagers are asked to choose for Jesus, camping experiences where students learn the power and necessity of a faith community, and teaching experiences where students must defend their faith are all crucial to long-term Christian growth.

Most teenagers doubt how strong or secure their faith is, and you have a vital part in spiritually encouraging them.

Four out of five said they've "really questioned" whether they were truly committed to Christ. And for many that time of great doubt came during their teenage years. Who helped them through those doubts? Friends, family members…and youth pastors.

As a youth leader, you have more influence and impact on teenagers' Christian faith than you realize.

When we asked these Christian college students who or what has been the biggest influence on their present commitment to Christ, youth leaders topped the list.

Barna's stats infer that many people come to Christ because they were part of a churchgoing family when they were children. But the key recommitment time—when they fully embraced or owned their faith—came when they were teenagers. And take a look at who you're serving God by loving day in and day out! So keep on keeping on…and God bless you.

Inviting Others

For those determined to reach teenagers for Christ and to help Christian teenagers share about their faith with others, the great gift of the National Study of Youth and Religion is "permission." Translation: The research results paint a picture of teenagers who are longing for something more in their lives and who are willing to hear about the exclusive claims of Christ.

Most of the teenagers who move into and out of your ministry have already been introduced to Jesus as children, but they need the powerful booster rockets that youth ministry offers to go the full distance—pouring their hearts and lives into an authentic, vulnerable, everyday, ultra-close-up relationship with him.

Jesus took his followers through many rounds of "evangelism"—that is, teaching them who he was and what he came to do and then inviting them into deeper relationship—before they made a life-and-death commitment to him.

And Jesus knew that if his disciples were going to learn how to invite others into a saving relationship with him, they'd have to learn by doing. First he trained them, then he sent them, and then he debriefed their experience to help them learn from it. Then he sent them again. That's not a formula, but it *is* a blueprint.

And you'll find some great additions to that blueprint in the pages that follow.

[SPECIAL EVENT]

Snack and Yak

Have students invite their friends to your group for a special "Snack and Yak" night—where there's plenty of good food and good conversation! Provide dinner or just snacks, and offer them to everyone.

Create a welcoming, comfortable atmosphere by playing music in the background and setting out lit candles. Invite people to sit down, eat, and talk about specific topics.

For example, SAY: **Come have a piece of pizza, and let's talk about friendship.**

Other topics to focus on in discussion are poverty, world hunger, dating, headline news and current events, goals, AIDS, homosexuality, and war.

You may provide some suggested questions to outline the discussion, but it may be even more effective to let the teenagers guide the conversation. This will be good practice for your students—after all, there are no scripts or question outlines in their everyday conversations with non-Christians.

The goal for your students is to simply create an environment of good food and good conversation—involving a lot of listening, praying, and relying on God for the right words to say. Your students' friends will feel welcome and listened to, your students will be able to appropriately share about a relationship with Jesus (and perhaps be challenged to think through everyday issues in fresh ways), and everyone will enjoy delicious food!

Afterward, discuss the experience with your students using these questions:

- **What did you enjoy most about tonight?**
- **What effect did a commitment to listening have on your conversation?**
- **In what ways were you able to naturally express something about your relationship with God?**
- **How can you rely on God to help you reach out to friends who don't yet have a close relationship with Jesus?**
- **How can you practice this kind of "snack and yak" on a regular basis in your own life?**

(MOVIE IDEA)

How Many Thumbs Up?

To help students reach out to their friends through shared experiences, do a four-week series called "At the Movies." Have students work together to set up your home or youth room like a movie theater, and provide popcorn and other fun snacks. Ask students to vote on a list you've created of 10 movies, and choose the movies by the majority's vote.

Then have your students invite their friends to watch each movie with the youth group. Afterward, either talk about the movie as a group or encourage your students to go to a coffee shop or restaurant with their friends and discuss the movie there. Suggest thought-provoking questions such as these:

- **What do you think the point of the movie was?**

- **Who do you think was the hero?**

- **Who did you most relate to? Why?**

- **If you could write the sequel, what part of the story would you continue? What would happen?**

Through this outreach idea, you'll equip your teenagers to take the initiative in spending time with friends, talking about important topics, and learning from one another.

If you want great ideas for exploring movies with your teenagers, try *Group's Blockbuster Movie Events* (see Appendix on page 222).

Soup Kitchen Potluck

Partner with a soup kitchen or homeless shelter for an entire year. Challenge your students to forgo the annual service trip and, instead, turn it into an ongoing part of their lives.

Ask the soup kitchen or homeless shelter staff how you could serve every week. Encourage students to build relationships with the people who are there rather than just remaining at a distance.

Afterward, get together and discuss these questions:

- **What would Jesus have done and said in your place? How did you follow his example? Explain.**

- **How did you follow—or not follow—Jesus' example of outreach?**

- **Why is it important that you are involved in this outreach for the long haul, not just one time? How is it difficult? enjoyable?**

- **How can you reach out to the people you're serving with Jesus' grace and love?**

Then pray together for the people you interacted with.

As a group, view this outreach relationship as a sort of "potluck": You bring the food, they bring the experiences, and everyone is fed.

[SERVICE IDEA 2]

All Expenses Paid

When you have an upcoming winter or summer retreat or service trip, ask your students which non-Christian friends they'd most like to invite. Spend regular time praying for these friends by name, asking God to make it possible for them to come along and grow closer to Jesus and other teenagers.

Each week, have your students give money toward retreat or trip scholarships. Set a goal (by dollars or by people) for how much you'd like to raise as a group. Along the way, talk with your students about why they gladly give money for their friends to attend. Discuss the kind of experiences your students hope their friends will have.

When you have enough money, give the OK for students to invite their friends by saying, "We'd like to pay for you because we'd really love for you to go." Not everyone may decide to attend, but many will.

Before going on the trip, discuss these questions with your students:

- **Why was it important for you to see this friend go on the trip?**
- **What were the important factors that led to this person coming along?**
- **How can we continue to pray for and serve this friend?**
- **How can we reflect Jesus' love with this person?**

Remind your students to pray for the non-Christians during the trip and to be trusted and accepting friends. Afterward, encourage the invited teenagers to check out other youth group events and get-togethers.

This experience will help your students intentionally serve and pray for their friends who may not be close to Jesus, as well as strengthen their own faith.

BONUS IDEA

Ask your church missions committee or people from the congregation to commit to matching the amount your students raise.

[OUTREACH IDEA 1]

Just Because

Find out how teenagers can use their skills, gifts, and interests to reach out to peers they may not usually interact with. With your students, brainstorm ways they can serve another group, club, or team at school or in the community.

Here are some ideas:

- washing uniforms
- attending a debate team's competition simply to show support
- helping to recruit people for a blood drive
- cleaning up the gym after a game
- supplying water to the track or cross country team
- chasing down balls for the tennis team's practice

When anybody asks why your students are doing this, encourage them to simply say that they serve because they care.

After each service experience, discuss these questions with your students:

- **How is selflessly serving others essential in our outreach to others?**
- **How can we continue to make serving others part of our youth group's DNA?**

BONUS IDEAS

JUST BECAUSE—Family Style

For a radical twist on the above activity, challenge your students to see how many random acts of kindness they can do for family members without getting caught. The gospel will be lived out right in your students' homes! Ideas could include these:

- doing a load of laundry
- washing the car
- making younger siblings their favorite snacks
- taking out the trash without being asked

JUST BECAUSE—Conference Style

As you plan for a retreat or conference your group is attending, call the volunteer coordinator of the conference. Offer your group's help in distributing programs, cleaning, setting up tables and chairs, or whatever else is needed.

[OUTREACH IDEA 2]

The Bigger Picture

Here are some ideas that will point your students toward people who are in need around the world. Choose any of these ideas that your students are drawn to and that best fit your youth group's passion for outreach.

- **Join a country**—Adopt a country or a people group somewhere in the world. Learn about it and pray for everything the people do there. Contact and partner with a specific church from the region, and ask about how you can encourage and serve them. Then do it!

- **Sponsor a child**—Partner with a group like World Vision or Compassion International, and commit to sponsoring a child together (or groups of about five students might each adopt a child). Seek to build a relationship between your group and this child. Learn about the child's culture, and pray for his or her health, happiness, and relationship with Jesus.

- **Go on a workcamp together**—Check out www.groupworkcamps.com, choose where you want to go together, and put your faith into action. You'll be involved in needed service projects, and you'll spend amazing times with God and teenagers from churches around the country.

- **Be prayer buddies with younger children**—Ask students to think back to when they were in second or third grade. Who were some of their heroes in the older grades? Why? Challenge each student to think of a younger child—a sibling, family friend, or neighbor—with whom he or she could be a prayer buddy. Encourage students to talk with the children's parents and ask permission to be prayer buddies. Remind students to pray frequently for and with these children and to give them fun notes or small gifts once in a while.

- **Work with Habitat for Humanity**—Arrange for your youth to spend a day with Habitat for Humanity. Habitat builds houses

continued on next page >>

The Bigger Picture
(continued)

all over the world with the express purpose of eliminating sub-standard housing. Look up Habitat in your local phone book, or find your nearest chapter online (www.habitat.org). Ask when and where their next projects are happening.

Members of your group can help build a nice house at all stages of the labor. The project is overseen by contractors, carpenters, plumbers, and other building professionals.

Gather the volunteers from your group to begin the workday with prayer and reflection. Read Matthew 7:24-27; 1 Corinthians 3:7-15; and Ephesians 2:19-22. Remember that the purpose of participating in this project is to offer a model of Christ's love through action. The gifts we give to others, even something as big as a house, will one day pass away. But the gift of love and life offered in Jesus is eternal.

During and after each outreach experience, discuss these questions:

- **How did this experience change the way you view others? God? yourself?**
- **When we do outreach to serve or care for others, what do you think *we* get out of it?**
- **What motivates you to continue reaching out to people in need?**
- **In what ways do you serve God by how you serve his children?**

[APPLICATION IDEA]

Dial

Teenagers may enthusiastically tell others about a relationship with Jesus, and they may be actively involved in outreach events. But there's another kind of "reaching out" that's necessary in a Christian teenager's life, and that's the kind that involves confession, forgiveness, and reconciliation within a relationship. If your students are harboring grudges or refusing to take steps to heal a friendship, they will be less able to clearly reflect Jesus' unconditional love and forgiveness.

First read Matthew 5:23-24 together: "So if you are presenting a sacrifice at the altar in the Temple and you suddenly remember that someone has something against you, leave your sacrifice there at the altar. Go and be reconciled to that person. Then come and offer your sacrifice to God."

In the middle of the room, have one cell phone for every five to 10 students.

SAY: **Before we begin to worship God tonight, I'd like us to take to heart what Jesus tells us in this passage.**

ASK:

- **What does God seem most about in these verses?**
- **How might we follow through on this as a group?**

SAY: **For us to be right with God, we've got to make things right with those around us. I'm going to give you a chance right now to make things right by calling someone—a friend, mom, dad, sister, or whoever—and say what you must say to make things right. You might apologize for how you've hurt that person, or you might explain how that person has hurt you and offer forgiveness. You may just ask some good questions.**

Allow up to half an hour for students to make their calls.

Afterward, debrief the experience. ASK:

- **What was it like to immediately put this passage into practice?**
- **How can you continue reaching out to people in your life?**

To end, have students form groups of three or four and pray together for their relationships. Congratulate students on their honesty and courage.

ministryTOOLS

A Window to My World

Use this idea to encourage students to look around and see where people are broken and hurting—and decide how they will reach out with God's love.

SAY: **Brokenness started in the Garden of Eden, when Adam and Eve ruined the possibility for perfect relationships—with God, with each other, and even with the rest of God's creation. After these first two people sinned, brokenness entered all human relationships.**

Give students notebooks and pens. Take your group to any public area, and give teenagers about 45 minutes to walk around and look for signs of brokenness in people's relationships with God, with one another, and with creation. Have students record their observations and then share their notes with the group when everyone gathers together again.

ASK:

- **How does brokenness affect people? friendships?**
- **How can our youth group reach out and help heal broken people?**
- **What will *you* do differently in light of the brokenness in the world?**

BONUS IDEA

You might also want to repeat the exercise and have students look for the reverse: Where do they see God using people to reflect renewal and peace?

Turning Up the Volume With No Words

Have your students brainstorm what it would be like to be outreach-oriented with their friends at school this week.

ASK:

- **What are the most creative and effective ways you can think of to share with your friends about a relationship with Jesus?**

See how many ideas you can come up with together in five minutes.

After all the ideas have been shared, have each student put a hand over his or her mouth. Tell students to imagine this hand over their mouths for the entire next week.

ASK:

- **What would remain on the list we just brainstormed?**
- **What items should be added if we can't use our mouths?**
- **What one idea will you use to tell others about a relationship with Jesus?**

Give students pens, and have them each write an idea on their hands as a way of committing to outreach with friends.

Our Message

Use this idea to explore how you can show the love of Jesus together as a group. Give each student five green sticky notes and five red sticky notes.

On the green notes, have students write ways your group gives people a good picture of who Jesus is and what he's about.

On the red notes, have students do the opposite and write how your group may give people the wrong picture of who Jesus is and what he's about.

If you're really brave, have the students who are newest to the group do this activity separately (make sure they know they will be anonymous). Then compare these responses to what your "older" students wrote.

When going over the responses together, concentrate on the positive things students wrote. Celebrate the things your group does to show the amazing love of Jesus to others.

Then choose one of the negative points (perhaps the one that came up most often), and talk together about how you might work on it. ASK:

- **Why do you think this is a weakness of ours?**
- **What can we do in this area to better reflect Jesus to people around us?**
- **What's the ultimate purpose of reaching out to people?**
- **How can we rely on God to help us show his love to others?**

SAY: **This experience demonstrates one of the best parts of being Christians together—celebrating what God is doing in us and asking God to continue to make us more like him.**

We care about what people are going through.

We gossip too much.

Errand Express

Encourage your students to look for outreach opportunities within your own church. One of those opportunities is serving elderly people who face daily challenges due to lack of mobility.

Some of the elderly people in your church might need help doing errands such as grocery shopping, while others may just need transportation to and from their home and the store. Have your students talk to people in the church and find out who needs what kind of help. Then have them create a monthly list or chart that details which teenager will serve which elderly person on which day. Or each student might commit to serving one person for the remainder of the year. Remind students to reach out to the people they're serving with love, patience, and flexibility.

You might want to have an ongoing Saturday tradition of meeting together, praying, and then separating to shop or assist with errands. Afterward, you can meet up again for lunch to discuss the experience. ASK:

- **What's it like for you to reach out to an older member of your church?**
- **What does your service mean to the person? How do you know?**
- **How does your attitude about outreach compare to the attitude God wants you to have? Explain.**
- **What motivates you to serve in this way?**
- **What are some other everyday ways you can serve others?**

Doing the Dirty Work

Give your students the opportunity to serve people whose long hours and hard work often go unrecognized—the janitors at your church. First have teenagers talk to the person who supervises the janitor or janitors at your church and ask what day would be easiest for your group to take over. Ask students to get a list of daily janitorial duties and to note where all the supplies are kept. Then have volunteers organize a day or weekend your group can take over the janitor's work at the church. Teenagers can sign up for one- to two-hour shifts, enough to make up a full eight-hour day. Students should assign duties from the list to each shift. Some will need to be repeated each shift, such as emptying the trash cans and checking the bathrooms for toilet paper and paper towels.

While you might be tempted to surprise the janitor with his or her day off, give advance notice so he or she can plan activities for the day and make notes for your volunteer janitors.

ASK:

- **What did this experience teach you about yourself? about outreach?**
- **What do you think God would say about the work you did? Explain.**
- **How has this outreach activity helped someone? encouraged someone? built friendship? pleased God?**
- **What are other ways you can acknowledge someone else's work and reach out in a tangible way?**

Suggested Resources

Here are some resources that explore outreach and will give you ideas for including it in your ministry:

- *Transformation Stations: Experiencing Jesus' Passion* (Group Publishing)
- *Thriving Youth Groups*, Jeanne Mayo (Group Publishing)
- *Group's Blockbuster Movie Illustrations: The Sequel*, Bryan Belknap (Group Publishing)
- *Ultimate Skits: 20 Parables for Driving Home Your Point*, Bryan Belknap (Group Publishing)
- *Mere Christianity*, C.S. Lewis
- *Ancient-Future Evangelism: Making Your Church a Faith-Forming Community*, Robert E. Webber
- *Jesus and the Disinherited,* Howard Thurman

Chapter 8

POST-
modernism

Caught in the Postmodern Crack?
by Rick Lawrence

One major tenet of postmodern life is a dogged determination to be inclusive and pluralistic. The National Study of Youth and Religion found that most American teenagers espouse a live-and-let-live view of religious differences. "Diversity and tolerance" are not only the primary religious tenets taught in public schools, but they're also the primary messages in most films and TV shows targeted at young people.

I don't believe it's a bad thing that schools and the media have so heartily embraced the postmodern "commandments." An owned, strengthened faith must be lived out in the world's marketplace of ideas and beliefs. Our job is to engage teenagers about what they hear and learn at school and in their entertainment—to teach them to be *critical thinkers* about everything they're taking in—not rescue them from the world.

The Lodo on Pomo

In our postmodern secular culture, exclusivity is at the top of the sin pyramid. For example, it's more than fine to talk about your commitment to Christ…as long as you recognize that your choice is just one of many equally valuable choices. That means the Gospel phrases "narrow gate," "the way," and "I am" are semi-scandalous—just as they were when the Pharisees first heard Jesus utter them. You have to walk gingerly around Christ's "exclusive" claims if you want to reach unchurched teenagers living in the postmodern age.

Or do you? The truth is, I think the previous paragraph may represent a quickly fading conventional wisdom.

I believe that many of today's millennial teenagers are literally sick of eating nonexclusionary "truths." They've been through the truth cafeteria line and gorged themselves, but they're still famished. They really like the "sweet beliefs" offered by their postmodern culture, but they've had so much of it that they're craving a nice slice of pot roast. They deep-down want real food (and I think that food is exclusive, capital-T truth) because they're simply not eating everything postmodernism is serving.

St. Louis Post-Dispatch journalist Colleen Carroll spent a year asking more than 500 young people what was drawing them to orthodox Christianity. The result is her book *The New Faithful: Why Young Adults Are Embracing Christian Orthodoxy* (Loyola Press).

Christianity Today asked Carroll why young people are so spiritually hungry.

"The hunger comes from a lot of different places," she responded. "If you feel like you weren't fed growing up, then you're going to have intense hunger. So some of it is just 'I didn't get what I need from my church.' "

Later in the interview, Carroll said teenagers are craving the "hard gospel"—that's not on the conventional soft-serve postmodern theological menu.

So what might the hard gospel look like in your ministry? You'll see lots of effective tools in the second part of this chapter; here are a few initial ideas to get your brain sparking.

Fill their environment with "raw truth" music.

In the past, I've labeled some contemporary Christian music "Trojan horse" stuff. Here's why. In the computer world, a Trojan horse is a "destructive program that masquerades as a benign application." Sometimes these programs offer to rid your computer of viruses, but instead they introduce destructive viruses.

To most parents, Christian music represents a welcome alternative to the grimy, disgusting mainstream music they hear spilling out of their teenagers' iPods and headphones. And in many cases, it is. But some of what's popular in today's Christian music has nothing to do with the real gospel.

Trojan-horse Christian music teaches that Jesus will make your life happy, fulfilled, and satisfying. That's fine, but tell that to thousands of Christ followers who will literally give up their lives for Jesus this year as martyrs for their faith. The Christian life was never portrayed as "shiny and happy" in the New Testament.

Today's teenagers gravitate to music that is gritty, raw, and emotional—it has the power to embrace their emotional realities. And the best Christian music does that, too. Look for music that is highly personal, raw, and intensely God-focused, and you'll hit a nerve with them.

Lead them into "raw truth" experiences.

There's a reason reality shows are so popular among young people. But it's sad and ironic that so many who are sick of "unreality" feel entertained by false reality. Give them the real thing because that's what they're really hungry for. Get your teenagers involved in anything that forces them to live out what they say they believe, and then watch them begin to embrace a new identity that has Christ at its center.

This means mission trips, service experiences, campus Bible groups, faith discussions at coffeehouses, youth-led worship groups, deliberate exposure to real people's hurt and brokenness...you name it. (Check out the National Network of Youth Ministries at www.youthworkers.net for ideas.)

The key in ministry to postmodern teenagers is to plunge them into God experiences and then make sure you do "cognitive debriefing" with them. Meaning, today's teenagers are transformed by "raw truth" experiences, but they desperately need a biblical context and purpose for those experiences. We used to teach first and then use that teaching as a launching pad for experiences. Now the experience is a launching pad for teaching. For more on this, check out Thom and Joani Schultz's *The Dirt On Learning* (Group Publishing).

Challenge them with the "raw truth" of Jesus.

The nice Jesus that we've concocted in an effort to "sell" teenagers Christianity is, well, boring to today's teenagers. John F. Kennedy mobilized a generation of young people who were a lot like your students with these words: "Ask not what your country can do for you; ask what you can do for your country." A loose youth ministry translation is this: "Tell not what God can do for your young people; tell them what they can do for God." There's entirely too much talk in today's church about what God "owes" us for following him. There's entirely too little attention given to his claims on us—the crucial mission and role he has for each of us.

Jesus gathered his followers with a curt "Follow me!" He told them most people were headed for destruction and only a few were walking through "the narrow door." He purposely baited the self-secure religious leaders of the day by calling them names and lampooning their ridiculous spiritual practices. He told those who were starting to believe he was the Messiah that they'd have to eat his flesh and drink his blood to have any part of him. When his best friend tried to get in his way, he called him "Satan" and shoved him aside.

And, most startling, while his disciples were waiting for him to change the world, he told them, "No, *you're* going to change the world—under my authority and with my strength." They went on to turn the world upside down with the gospel.

In short, Jesus made both his enemies and friends uncomfortable with his actions and claims. And, as he said, "Go and do the same."

Show them that the "raw truth" about life is all about "congruence."

My friend and pastor, Tom Melton, once told me the key to living passionately for Christ is something he calls congruence. Basically, he's talking about truth in advertising—live your commitment to Christ in all the details of your life, not just in selected environments or situations. When you do, you'll experience an exponential increase in your influence and impact on those around you. How will your students learn congruence? Well, when what they see backs up what they hear.

Whenever we speak about our strongly held beliefs, we must ask ourselves if our spouses, parents, or closest friends could stand and testify that we've lived what we're urging others to do. If not, then we're not congruent. We're posers and schemers and con artists.

Surround your students with congruent adults—no matter what age they are—and you'll start to set a "new norm" in them. Congruent adults plant seeds inside teenagers' souls that say, "No matter what I see or hear or experience, I know God's best is possible for me—I have no excuses. And by the grace of God, I can do it!"

Teenagers need us to lead them into experiences that are congruent to their nature and God's nature. It's in those experiences that they see more clearly what God meant them to be from the foundation of time.

Give them opportunities to artistically express the "raw truth."

Today's teenagers intrinsically know that the Godless worldview is sorely lacking in satisfaction and truth. They're longing for "miracle and mystery," and one way to connect them to these is to set them loose to express themselves artistically.

Jonny Baker is someone who provides "miracle and mystery" moments where teenagers can closely connect with God. He is the co-creator of the widely used prayer experience for youth groups called *The Prayer Path* and the similar multimedia event resource *Worshipping the Creator*. He is also a leader in the "alternative worship" movement in England.

Jonny and others combine creative forces to set up engaging and surprising worship spaces. For instance, they drape an old Anglican church with sheets, sectioning off a portion of the sanctuary. They use shadowy lighting, dance-track music, sculpture, poetry, experiential activities, installation art, video images, and PowerPoint slides to invite people into worship. The experience prods participants to express themselves artistically—to move toward God actively.

What's reflected here is this truth: At the core of artistic expression is something Christ-like. God spoke into a void and created. Every artist knows what that feels like: Between nothing and something is an act of faith. And more than anything else, today's teenagers are drawn to risk-taking, faith-demanding artistic challenges.

So encourage your students to artistically express their faith and grow closer to God through their specific talents. Consider forming "artistic teams" of students who are set free to translate your meeting or event theme into multimedia presentations, experiential activities, dance, poetry, drama, film, and visual arts. And recruit a few students to transform your environment every week into a surprising, inviting space.

Make sure your messages are designed to deliver the "raw truth."

It's rare you'll find a youth minister who doesn't use some kind of sermon strategy as a fail-safe way to communicate the gospel to teenagers. The "youth talk"—usually featuring one-way communication, without any participation or interaction from the ones being talked to—is the quintessential cross-denominational ministry practice.

However, there's a mountain of research that discounts one-way lecturing as an effective method for helping people, especially young people, learn. But that's not all. Even if you're a big believer in youth talks, you likely can't point to a sermon or message that actually changed your life. Life change is almost always the result of an experience followed by some kind of debriefing.

And youth leaders seem to agree with this. When we asked youth ministers around the world to tell us how they teach their students spiritual truths, "youth talks or messages" ranked dead last in a list of six strategies—only 5 percent made sermons their top choice. Even so, we know from our own ongoing research that seven out of 10 youth leaders include a sermon as one element of a typical youth group meeting.

So here are some ways to revitalize or replace sermons to communicate the gospel to postmodern teenagers. In addition, try using helpful resources such as *Essential Messages for Youth Ministry*, which offers active, experiential messages.

- **Inject small-group discussions into your message time.** If something meaningful happens but you keep barreling through the talk, it will be lost. Give students plenty of time to process what they've just seen, heard, learned, or experienced.

- **Engage students with experiential learning activities before,**

during, or after the talk. Set up your messages with activities that surprise and entice students into the truth. This way, instead of telling them what to think, they're making the connections for themselves. That makes life application a lot more powerful...and lasting.

- **Use games, media, drama, or object lessons to spark discussion.** Use movie clips, skits, themed games, and even visual illustrations to kick off a discussion that flows into a youth talk. Including some kind of media is an effective way to grab teenagers' attention.

- **Send students on group explorations.** Have students form groups, and send them on a mission to experience or discover something together. They'll have many intriguing insights and lots of fun interacting and exploring together.

- **Lead them into out-of-building experiences.** Work hard to connect gospel learning to teenagers' real-world experiences. Set up experiences that will help teenagers *know* what God is like, not just know about what God is like. Service projects and mission trips are catalysts for this.

Recognize the "raw truth" of this generation—belonging before believing.

Most churches essentially require young people to "clean up their act" and learn to behave like mature Christians before they're welcomed into the fellowship. But it should be the other way around—teenagers will welcome a relationship with Christ *after* someone welcomes them into a community of loving Christians. Good relationships with others are the faith starting point for many teenagers, so focus on helping students belong before expecting them to believe.

Engage in Experiences

Leonard Sweet says postmodern culture is characterized by a "back to the future" mentality. In medieval times, he says, people had a keen understanding that they were more than just physical bodies with brains and emotions—they understood that human beings have "souls."

Sweet says, "We're living in one of the greatest rediscoveries of the soul in the last thousand years, and it's totally taken place outside of Christianity. Well, why? We're totally not understanding what the soul is about for postmoderns—it's relationships and rituals…This is the difference between modern and postmodern ministry. One asks, 'What do you think?' It tries to help kids think the right thoughts. The other asks, 'What do you feel? What are you experiencing?' It tries to create rites and rituals that can help bring about right experiences."

Looking for ways to engage students in experiences that help them learn God's truths? Read on…

[SERVICE IDEA]

Wash My Feet

Engage your students with activities that challenge them to take risks in friendship and treat others as Jesus did. Try this: Set out a basin of water and a towel (more for a larger group), and have everyone sit in a circle. ASK:

- **How well do you think we know one another? Give examples.**
- **How well do you think we treat one another? Give examples.**

Have students share their different perspectives on how well the members of your group know and treat one another. ASK:

- **How can we get to know one another better?**
- **How can we treat one another better?**

Listen for specific answers, and cue in on answers that touch on the idea of taking risks in friendship and getting out of personal comfort zones.

SAY: **Sitting in a circle week after week won't necessarily bring us closer together. Sometimes we need to venture out of our own personal zones and take some risks—which can be really uncomfortable. But Jesus did this all the time with people! We'll get to that in a second. First, I'd like all of you to take off your shoes and socks. What each of us will do now is wash the feet of another person in the group.**

Model by kneeling before a student and asking, "May I wash your feet?" If the student gives permission, proceed to dip his or her feet in the water and wipe them dry.

Let this student now do the same for another person.

Continue in silence until everyone has had the opportunity to wash someone's feet and have his or her own feet washed.

Have a volunteer read aloud John 13:1-17. ASK:

- **How did this experience make you feel?**
- **How do you think the disciples felt when Jesus washed their feet? Why?**
- **What do you think the purpose was of what Jesus was doing?**
- **Besides washing feet, in what ways can you take a risk to treat someone the way Jesus would?**

"Today in the News" Prayer

Your students probably know a lot about why they should be in constant prayer for people around the world, but they may not have a lot of opportunities to actually experience this. Help make worldwide concerns and needs more emotionally and spiritually real to them through this activity.

Gather a bunch of newspapers, and spread them all over the floor. Scatter tea lights or battery-operated "candles" all over the newspapers. Turn out the lights so that certain parts of the newspaper are more visible in the light while others are more in the dark.

Gather your group outside the room where you've set out newspapers.

Have a volunteer read 1 Thessalonians 5:17 aloud. ASK:

- **What do you think Paul means when he tells us to "never stop praying"?**
- **How would you describe your own prayer life?**

After several responses, SAY: **We can live this verse if we never stop praying as we look around our world. I'd like you to quietly enter this room. Approach a newspaper, read an article, touch the article with your hand, and pray for what you think God might want in this situation.**

Allow up to half an hour for students to pray over the newspapers. Afterward, gather together for private reflection and a time of worship. ASK:

- **What discoveries, if any, did you have during this time of prayer?**
- **What kinds of things did you realize you should never stop praying for?**
- **What kind of impact will praying for others have on you and your relationship with God?**

Finish by praying. SAY: **God, help us to not live in this world without seeing those situations for which you want us to pray. Always help us lift up others in prayer to you. Thank you for your love, for your power, and for all you do in our world. Help us follow you always. Amen.**

[PRAYER IDEA 2]

Look at Me...Pray for Me

Our prayer and worship can be so individualistic that we may lose sight of the purpose of community, even when we're physically together. It's mostly through relationships and community that your students will learn about prayer and worship—and about a relationship with Jesus. Try this idea for helping students experience prayer and worship as "relationship" experiences.

Have students gather in pairs. Explain to them that this might seem a bit uncomfortable, but you'd like them to pray for each other while they look each other directly in the eye. Encourage them not to look away as they focus on talking to God.

Allow time for students to pray with and for each other. Expect some uncomfortable laughter, but also expect students to rise to the challenge and intimately connect with God together. Afterward, ASK:

- **What was this like? Explain.**

- **How important are we in one another's lives? in one another's relationships with God?**

- **In what ways can we support one another spiritually while still putting God first?**

You might want to repeat the same experience with a few worship songs; have everyone stand in a circle and worship God as a unified group. Encourage students to enjoy seeing one another praise God.

[MOVIE IDEA]

Youth Group at the Movies

Encourage your teenagers to think critically and with a faith filter about the pop culture they take in. When they learn to explore all entertainment with an eye for how it connects to what God values, they'll begin to live out their faith in Jesus on a daily basis.

Take one month to watch four movies together as a group. After each movie, take turns reviewing the movie either verbally or in writing.

To create these reviews, have students think critically about the characters, messages, themes, and artistic value of the movie.

Use these questions as a guide:

- **What stood out to you most from the movie?**
- **Which character did you most relate to? Why?**
- **What might God think of the movie? Explain.**
- **What Bible stories or verses does this movie remind you of?**
- **From watching the movie, what would someone learn about faith? grace? God? relationships? love? service? commitment?** (Change these to fit the specific film.)

Also as a group, come up with more discussion questions that would prompt people to consider the movie's message and how it aligns with what God values. Have students discuss these questions with friends.

Use Ministry and Media (www.ministryandmedia.com) as a resource for exploring media and culture through a biblical filter. Also be sure to incorporate parental support and a parent's form prior to these events.

BONUS IDEA

Napoleon Dynamite is a great movie to watch with your students. Napoleon Dynamite, the main character, is a high school student struggling to define his identity in a world of bullies, geeks, family quirks, and social awkwardness. While managing his relationships with his brother and the neighbor girl, he takes on the great challenge of helping his friend Pedro run for student-body president.

Youth Group at the Movies
(continued)

BONUS IDEAS

After watching the movie together, debrief using these questions as a guide:

- **How realistic or unrealistic is this movie in depicting high school? Explain.**
- **With what in this movie did you most identify? Why?**
- **Which character did you relate to most? Why?**
- **In your experience, what's the toughest part of being a teenager? How do you deal with this challenge?**
- **What role does God play in your life? in your unique identity?**
- **How can God make you free to be yourself?**

[SPECIAL MEETING IDEA]

Walk a Mile in My Shoes

Hearing others' stories is a powerful way for students to connect to God's heart, so make storytelling a common element in your youth ministry.

Instead of merely talking about the struggles in the world, invite people to join your group and share their personal stories. You might bring in a single parent, a recovering alcoholic, a pregnant teenager, someone struggling with depression, or someone who's been seriously injured.

Have students take some time to interview your visitors with whatever questions they'd like to ask. Afterward, ASK:

- **What did you learn from these stories?**
- **What does it mean to for us to "walk in someone else's shoes"?**
- **Now that we've heard stories firsthand, what kinds of actions can we take?**
- **Why is it important for us to tell _our_ stories to others?**

Pray together for each person who's taken the time to talk to your group, and ask God to heal all people who are struggling or hurting, including the people in your group.

A Text Without a Context

Here's a way to move students past a nice, agreeable view of God toward the "raw truth" about who Jesus really is and what it means to know him.

Dive together into complete portions of God's Word, rather than looking at just one or two verses at a time. You might do this by committing the entire semester or year to studying one book of the Bible together.

Make this an exciting and meaningful adventure for your students by coming up with ways you can immerse yourselves in Scripture. You might find ways to embrace—or even re-enact—the geography, culture, and way of life of the real people who wrote each portion of God's Word. Since reflection and interpretation are important steps to growing in faith, take the time to really dive into the Scripture instead of jumping straight to the application.

Once teenagers have explored God's Word patiently, holistically, and experientially, they'll naturally make the connections between the "raw truths" about God to the way they live their lives. Frequently discuss what you're exploring, using questions such as these:

- **What did you take away from this passage?**
- **Why is it important for you to dig into God's Word?**
- **How has your view of God changed? stayed the same?**
- **How will the truth about Jesus draw you closer to him?**

Turn Up the Radio

Think you know your students well? really well? To dig into the fascinating people who are your teenagers, do this activity with your entire ministry team. Because you'll more clearly understand your teenagers, you'll be able to better love them, serve them, and guide them to a relationship with Jesus.

Have your students work together to create a list of the top five to 10 most popular songs at the moment (these can be Christian or secular). They must all agree on the song choices! Then explore this list at your next volunteer or youth leader meeting. Go over the lyrics of each song, and listen to them if possible.

Talk about these questions as a ministry team:

- **What themes or points stand out from the songs? Why are these important to our ministry to youth?**
- **What truths do we find in these songs that we can discuss with our students?**
- **What can we learn about our students from their interest in these songs?**
- **What do these songs teach us about our students' world? view on life? relationships? future?**
- **After exploring these songs, how might we better serve and love our students—and why?**

End by praying for the songs' artists and for your teenagers.

[MESSAGE IDEA]

Message From Me

Give students a chance to take ownership over their own faith by having them share about God's truths with one another.

Hold a "Message From Me" night, where all students come prepared to express something about God and faith. This could be a truth they've discovered, an impression they want to share, or something they're struggling with.

Students should use their gifts in various ways, whether through music, drama, poetry, sculpture, paint, dance, or story. However, make it clear that this isn't the same as a "talent night." The point is to express something true about Jesus in creative and uniquely personal ways.

After everyone has had the opportunity to share something with the group, thank everyone, and then have time of prayer, reflection, and small-group discussion. ASK:

- **What was it like to share your "message" with the group?**

- **What did you learn about God from everybody else?**

- **What do we know that's true about Jesus and faith in Jesus?**

- **How can we express these truths to other people in our lives using our gifts and talents?**

I See Dead People

In your youth group times, regularly explore stories of historical Christians. Study these people's lives and accomplishments, and discuss together. By introducing students to these heroes of the faith tradition, you're helping them take part in a story and legacy that's bigger than any of us.

Some historical Christians you might explore are:

- C.S. Lewis
- Brother Andrew
- Corrie Ten Boom
- Mother Teresa
- Martin Luther
- J.R.R. Tolkien
- Harriet Tubman
- Fanny Crosby
- Dietrich Bonhoeffer
- Martin Luther King, Jr.
- St. Francis of Assisi
- St. Augustine
- Thomas Aquinas
- John Wesley

After exploring together, discuss these types of questions:

- **How does this person help you understand Christianity more clearly?**
- **How are you inspired to grow in your faith in Jesus?**
- **How does studying the stories and words of Christian "heroes" impact your life?**

When We Drop the Ball...

This activity's a little messy. But then again, that's sort of the point. Try this out to help your students engage with the "raw truth" about sin and how it affects us.

Set a children's pool full of water in the center of the room, and have students stand around it (or you could go to a local body of water and stand near the edge). Now give two students each a big red rubber ball.

Tell them to throw the balls into the water whenever they're ready.

Now ask two more students to take out the rubber balls and do the same thing, then two more students, and so on until everybody has had a chance to throw the balls into the water.

This activity will escalate until students are throwing the balls in such a way that people are getting splashed.

Have everyone stop and sit down around the pool (or near the water). ASK:

- **What was this experience like?**
- **How did you react to being splashed?**
- **How is this experience like real life?**
- **In what ways do you see people making messes?**
- **How are you being "splashed" in your life right now?**
- **How do we often try to avoid being "splashed"? What happens?**

SAY: **One commonly told story is of a person who was asked, "What's wrong with the world?" The person responded, "I am."**

continued on next page >>

When We Drop the Ball
(continued)

ASK:

- **Do you agree or disagree with this? Explain.**
- **How might what you do or say harm others?**
- **How do you react when someone's sin harms you?**

SAY: **Our sin affects others' lives. Our own sin makes a mess of the world; because we live as one big interconnected community, our actions never stay isolated.**

Talk about how this understanding affects our personal connection with our church community, our whole community, and the globe. Discuss what it means to take responsibility to serve others and be globally minded.

[EXPERIENTIAL WORSHIP IDEA]

Active Silence

Your students are busy and may rarely experience silence in their everyday lives, and they may incorporate silence into their relationships with Jesus even more rarely. Help them understand the value of "active" silence in worshipping God by leading them through two or three experiences.

Write one "worship" Scripture passage on a slip of paper (you'll need slips for all students). Include passages that explore the kind of sincere and wholehearted worship God wants from us. Here are some examples: Psalm 63:2-3; Psalm 95:6; John 4:23-24; Romans 12:10-13; Ephesians 5:19-20; Philippians 2:9-11; Hebrews 13:15-16; James 4:7-10; Revelation 4:8-11.

Also set out a set of disposable earplugs and a cushion or pillow for each student.

SAY: **Silence is important for living our faith because it helps us intentionally focus on God without any distractions. Basically, it brings us into** a more intimate relationship with Jesus. We can actually worship God through "active" silence, in which we are quiet before him but open to hear God's "still small voice" (1 Kings 19:12, King James Version)—those things he tells or shows us that we aren't as able to hear in the loudness of everyday life. Let's practice this type of worship right now.

Give each student a slip of paper, a cushion or pillow, and a set of earplugs. Ask students to each find a private spot in your meeting area where they can focus on God in silence.

SAY: **You'll spend the next half-hour worshipping and praying to God. Put away outside distractions, and let the earplugs block out any noises. Try to avoid talking to God about what you want or need. He cares about those things, but for now the goal is to come before God with a still heart and mind and receive the peace, encouragement, message of love, or Scripture that he wants to give you.**

For the next half hour, students will spend time in silent prayer and worship before God.

You may also want to provide Bibles, notebooks, and pens or pencils so students can quietly journal their thoughts and prayers.

After the time is up, bring everyone together.

SAY: **Even though you haven't spoken any words aloud, know that God hears and receives your prayers.**

You may want to end your time in silence as well, simply dismissing everyone. However, you might discuss the experience using these types of questions:

- **What was this experience like for you?**
- **How easy or difficult was it to worship God in this way?**
- **How might regularly worshipping God through silence impact your relationship with him?**
- **In what ways can you incorporate "active" silence into your faith and relationship with God?**

[ART IDEA]

Artistic Expression

Help students explore the Bible and express their response to God through art. Ask students to bring whatever artistic tools they wish to use—pencil, watercolor, clay, digital camera, oil paints, and so on—to your next meeting. Together, read one or several Bible passages you've decided on as a group.

(A great option would be Jesus' journey to the cross in Matthew 26:17-75; 27:1-50.)

When you've finished reading the passage or passages, ask your students to create works of art expressing that piece of Scripture and what it means to them. For example, Matthew 26:36-46 could be anything from a full-scale drawing of Jesus in the garden to a photo of hands praying.

When students have finished their art pieces, bring the group back together. Ask your artists to explain what they created and why.

ASK:

- **What was it like for you to explore the Bible passage in this way?**

- **What new meaning did this activity bring to the passage you explored? to God's Word in general?**

- **How did this experience bring you closer to Jesus?**

- **In what other ways can you use gifts and talents to study God's Word and grow in a relationship with Jesus?**

Close with a time of prayer, thanking God for the gift of Scripture and what it means for each person in your group.

Be sure to display the students' art somewhere in your church so parents and the rest of the congregation can appreciate it.

(MUSIC IDEA)

A Song for Me

Here's an experience that will lead teenagers to creatively explore their thoughts and feelings about faith and grow in their relationships with God.

Ask students to bring to your time together songs that they think best represent their faith and relationship with God (whether intimate, growing, weak, or nonexistent). Let your students know that the song can be secular or sacred, popular or classic; however, it must be appropriate for the group to listen to together. A student's song might have lyrics that mirror his or her thoughts on spiritual life, or the song can reflect what the student wants his or her relationship with God to be like. Or perhaps the song is meaningful for another reason.

At the following meeting, have individuals take turns playing and sharing about their song. If you have a large group, have students form groups of five to seven so everyone gets a turn (be sure to provide enough CD players, or have students bring players from home).

After all students have shared their songs, ASK:

- **What do you feel and think when you hear your song? Why?**
- **What does your song reveal about your thoughts on spiritual life and faith?**
- **In what ways is your faith story one-of-a-kind just as your song is one-of-a-kind?**
- **How does your song reflect your current relationship with God?**
- **Are you happy or unhappy about your current relationship with God? Explain.**
- **If you could change or highlight any of the lyrics of your song, what would you choose, and why?**
- **What thoughts or feelings about faith should you express to God?**
- **How will you approach God about your faith and relationship with him?**

continued on next page >>

ministryTOOLS

A Song for Me
(continued)

BONUS IDEA

In addition to having students bring their own songs, you may also choose the music you'll explore together as a group. You can do this occasionally or as a month-long series on music, faith, and spiritual themes. Choose songs that will lead to meaningful conversations about faith, God, life, and relationships. Great options may include music by artists such as U2, Sufjan Stevens, Jars of Clay, Andy Hunter, Jeremy Camp, Coldplay, Matchbox Twenty, Norah Jones, the David Crowder Band, Audioslave (particularly the album *Out of Exile*), Switchfoot, Relient K, the White Stripes, Handel's *Messiah*, Ben Harper and the Blind Boys of Alabama, and so on. Choose music that you feel is appropriate and relevant for your group.

After listening to select songs or even an entire album together, discuss the following with your students:

- **How does this music affect you emotionally? Why?**

- **What does this music have to say about God? truth? love? hope? forgiveness? sin?**

- **What view of God does this music set forth? Do you agree or disagree?**

- **How might music help lead you closer to Jesus? Give an example.**

- **How might music help lead you away from Jesus? Give an example.**

[RESOURCES]

Suggested Books

- *Essential Messages for Youth Ministry* (Group Publishing)

- *Transformation Stations: Surrendering My Life to God* (Group Publishing)

- *Worshipping the Creator,* Proost (Group Publishing)

- *Diving Deep: Experiencing Jesus Through Spiritual Disciplines,* Amy Simpson (Group Publishing)

- *The Younger Evangelicals: Facing the Challenges of the New World*, Robert E. Webber

- *Jesus Freaks,* DC Talk and The Voice of the Martyrs

- *The Way of the Heart: Desert Spirituality and Contemporary Ministry*, Henri J.M. Nouwen

Suggested Web Sites

- www.rejesus.co.uk/spirituality/index.html

- www.alternativeworship.org (alternative worship)

- http://web.ukonline.co.uk/paradigm/index.htm (online labyrinth)

ministryTOOLS

Appendix

Friendship First

EASY TO PLAN AND LEAD!

13 get-togethers use the proven magnetism of food to help everyone build friendships with one another and God. This tasty program is flexible for any church size or setting—and is sure to cook up a genuine culture of community in your church!

Youth Ministry Kit:

Kit includes:

- 8 participant books
- 1 DVD
- 1 leader guide
- 1 CD

Visit www.FriendshipFirst.com to find out more.

Church-wide kit also available

Transformation Stations:

Committing My Relationships to God
Experiencing Jesus' Passion
Giving My Time to God
Surrendering My Life to God

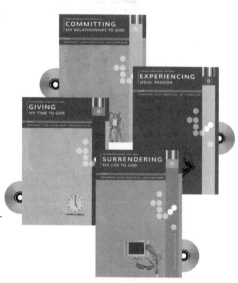

Guide teens through a reflective, media-rich experience that inspires them to give all of themselves to God, commit to worshipping him…and be transformed. Multisensory station lead participants through intriguing object lessons that help them know God at a deeper level. Includes a CD packed with powerful images, music & narration, Scripture connections, and customizable options.

it: Innovative Tools for Youth Ministry

EASY TO INSTALL—EASY TO USE!
MAKES BUILDING LESSONS A SNAP

Crack open this vault of ministry ideas and make big—and small events—meaningful and memorable. IT is incredible! 1,500 pages of life-changing ideas and a whopping 350 topics—selected by youth workers—give practical, creative tools for all levels of youth ministry. Every idea is included on customizable, cutting-edge software by LabOra®. Search by topic, Scripture, Bible character, and activity type.

Includes:

- Bible studies
- Games
- Quotations
- Prayer ideas
- Skits
- Worship ideas
- Devotions
- Movie clip discussion starters
- Music discussion starters
- Service projects
- Recommended Web sites
- And more!

Friendzee:

Christian Character
Close Connections

Explore the Bible through this wacky board game! Teenagers dive into spiritual topics and build close friendships as they enjoy fun, creative game-play. As they dig into Scripture, teens tell stories, sculpt clay, write, sketch, perform charades, and more. Great for up to 10 players. No supplies or preparation needed.

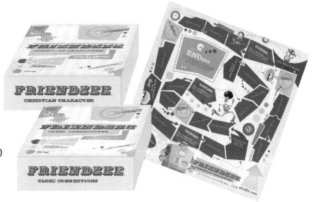

Blockbuster Movie Illustrations
Blockbuster Movie Illustrations, the Sequel
Blockbuster Movie Illustrations, the Return
Blockbuster Movie Events

Reel in teenagers by using clips from popular movies to vividly illustrate what the Bible has to say about critical issues they face. These clips work great as attention-getting openings, memorable closings, starting points to build a lesson on, and sermon illustrations.

Blockbuster Movie Events includes plans for 12 movie event nights, retreats, or holidays. You get discussion questions, games, activities, and decoration ideas for each movie. *Movie clips not included.*

Prayer Path

Journey through a multimedia labyrinth. Participants are guided by a CD that soars with provocative, devotional narration set against a worshipful music backdrop. Eleven stations lead participants to let go of busyness, center their lives on God, and reach out to the world with Christ's love.

Each kit includes a Leader Guide, 10 Participant Guides, 6 narrative CDs, and 2 videos.

Walking in His Footsteps

This intense multimedia worship adventure gives participants a personal and powerful grasp of the incredible sacrifice and glorious victory won on the cross.

Guided by a dramatic narrative on CD, teens move through 12 interactive, multi-sensory stations.

Worshipping the Creator

Take participants on a journey through creation using the book of Genesis, original poetic narratives, prayer, and reflection. Participants rotate through 8 stations, focusing on an aspect of creation at each station.

Includes 1-hour DVD of creation images, 6 CD audio guides, 10 Participant Guides, 7 full-color posters, and more.

Check Out the Entire Series!

Order today at www.group.com
or call 1.800.747.6060 ext. 1370

Also available at your favorite Church Resource Supplier